monsoonbooks

THE BOAT

Born in 1914, Walter Gardiner Gibson enlisted as a young soldier with the Argyll and Sutherland Highlanders. It was with their 2nd Battalion that he was sent to Asia, serving in India, China and Malaya for seventeen years.

His remarkable experiences during World War II include fighting in the Battle of Slim River, escaping through the Malayan jungle and surviving in a lifeboat for twenty-six days amidst cannibalism, desperation and treachery.

For two years he endured a Japanese prisoner-of-war camp in Medan until being liberated in Singapore in 1945. Often described as a colourful character, he wrote about his experiences in two books, *The Boat* and *Highland Laddie*.

After leaving the Army, he emigrated to Ontario, Canada, with his family.

Soldier, prisoner of war and author, Walter Gibson died on 24 March 2005, aged ninety.

T0154785

THE BOAT

SINGAPORE ESCAPE
CANNIBALISM AT SEA

WALTER GIBSON

monsoon

First published in print in 1952 by W.H. Allen & Co Ltd.
Republished in print in 2007 by Monsoon Books.

ISBN (paperback): 978-981-05-8301-9
ISBN (ebook): 978-981-4358-95-8

The publisher wishes to thank Mavis Hamilton (née Gibson)
for her kind assistance.

Cover photograph copyright©Getty Images.

Monsoon Books Pte Ltd
150 Orchard Road #07-02
Orchard Plaza
Singapore 238841
www.monsoonbooks.com.sg

Visit www.monsoonbooks.com.sg to learn more about all our books.

Printed in USA

To my wife, Mary, my daughter, Ree, and my son, Colin Roy,

but for whom this story would never have been told.

My thanks are due to MacDonald Daly, the writer, whose untiring efforts

shaped my war experiences into their present form;

and to David Emsley for his constructive criticism and unfailing

encouragement.

1

My name is Gibson. Walter Gibson, formerly of the Argyll and Sutherland Highlanders, with whose 2nd Battalion I served for seventeen years in India, China and Malaya.

This story, as I plan it, will be completed on 2 March 1952—for that will be the tenth anniversary of the morning I climbed into the boat.

I write this chronicle—of the days of horror which I and Doris Lim, the Chinese girl, endured together in the boat—because from all over the world, during the last two years, have come letters demanding that I should do so.

Late in 1949 my story, in briefer form, was told in a British Sunday newspaper.

As a sequel it was published, though still more briefly, in nearly all the tongues of the world. It appeared in newspapers and magazines in Europe, the United States, China, Japan and South America.

Reader's Digest translated it into French, German, Spanish, Dutch, Italian, Danish, Swedish and Japanese.

And from all those countries, in all those tongues, have come requests from people who want to know more.

It is given to few, thank God, to drift for a month beneath a pitiless blazing sun, across 1,000 miles of ocean with nothing but a few handfuls of food and a few mouthfuls of water to sustain them during that time.

It is given to fewer still to be the only white survivor of such an ordeal.

And never again, I pray, may it be given to one man, as it was to me, to be the only white survivor of 135 souls who, on that morning of 2 March 1942, looked to the boat for salvation.

Four days before, the 1,000-ton Dutch K.P.M. steamer *Rooseboom*, with a crew of Dutch officers and Javanese seamen, left the port of Padang in Sumatra. She was carrying more than 500 evacuees from Malaya, most of them British.

Singapore had fallen to the Japanese. The evacuees included soldiers of many ranks, officials, policemen, traders, miners, planters, women and children.

The *Rooseboom* was taking them, crowded in her cabins and on her decks, to Ceylon and safety. There it was hoped that the regiments broken in the Malaya debacle would be formed again.

At midnight on Sunday, 1 March, the *Rooseboom* was torpedoed halfway to Ceylon. She sank in a few minutes. Only one of her boats was launched and kept afloat.

Towards it swam and paddled survivors. Eighty of them scrambled or were lifted into the boat. More than fifty others clung to the side.

The lifeboat was twenty-eight feet long and only eight feet at its widest part. The number of people it had been built to hold was twenty-eight.

For over a thousand miles, taking twenty-six days, she drifted across the Indian Ocean. Drama, tragedy, heroism, murder, pathos and self-sacrifice went with her day by day.

In the end, when the boat pounded on a coral island less than a hundred miles from the port of Padang from which the *Rooseboom* had sailed, only four people survived.

Two were Javanese sailors, whose final dreadful deeds aboard the boat made them unworthy of the life which was restored to them. The third was a Chinese girl, Doris Lim, who had worked for British Intelligence against the Japanese.

And I was the other.

I had fought with the Argylls, from last ditch to last ditch, in the bitter Malaya campaign of December 1941 and January 1942.

I had survived a six-week escape through the jungle after the Battle of Slim River.

I had crossed to Sumatra in a sampan and had joined up there with fellow Argylls and other troops before boarding the *Rooseboom*.

I had been asleep on a mattress on the *Rooseboom*'s deck when the torpedo struck.

But let me begin at the beginning ...

2

The docks and harbour of Padang, the Sumatran port, presented a grim sight in the days which immediately succeeded the fall of Singapore.

The town itself was crowded with people who had escaped from Malaya. The Japanese were bombing systematically.

The *Rooseboom*, usually engaged on the coastal run between Sumatra and Java, had been en route from Batavia to Ceylon and safety when she was ordered to pick up evacuees at Padang.

Now, deep down in the water from the human load she was carrying, she drew away from the quayside and we could see the half-submerged ships—victims of the Jap raid—which dotted the entrance to the harbour.

Even so, I found myself caught up in the spell of the sunset's beauty—for the dying rays fell on lush tropical vegetation on the dozens of islands about us. There are few more beautiful harbour approaches in the world than Padang's answer to Bremerhaven.

Behind me a voice said, 'It's lovely, Hoot, isn't it?' and I turned to find Willie MacDonald by my elbow.

Sergeant Willie MacDonald was an old friend of mine. He had been wounded with the Argyll carrier platoon at Dipang, but had remained on duty until the battle was over. He had come out of hospital to join in the fighting on Singapore, and had escaped to Sumatra.

'Aye, it's lovely, Toorie,' I answered him. 'The folks at home would give a bit to see this, wouldn't they?'

'Gie me Inverness,' said Willie. 'And the Caledonian Canal.'

It was a scrap of conversation I will never forget—the words of a brave Highlander, many years away from home, but with his heart still in the silver city he was never to see again.

The atmosphere aboard the *Rooseboom* was a strange mixture of relief at leaving the perils of Malaya and Singapore behind, and of tension at the ever-present prospect of bombs and torpedoes.

A Jap plane had been over the port not long before we left, and we scanned the skies anxiously, our two Bren guns mounted.

The troops were packed like sardines and sleeping on deck almost on top of one another.

But after the Dutch captain had issued a bulletin that we were now out of bombing range, and two nights had passed without an event, tension lessened, everyone became more friendly and the atmosphere was very nearly carefree.

The senior army officer aboard the ship was Brigadier Archie Paris, who had commanded the division against hopeless odds during the Malayan campaign.

He and the brigade major, Major Angus MacDonald, member

of a famous Argyllshire family and heir to a £200,000 estate, had escaped from Singapore in a yacht owned and sailed by a young officer of the Argylls, Captain Mike Blackwood.

Blackwood, red-haired and blue-eyed, was a tremendously keen yachtsman. He had won several races while we were stationed in Singapore before the campaign.

He, the brigadier and Major MacDonald were all engaged in the hand-to-hand fighting as Singapore fell.

At one stage about fifty Jap tanks threatened to penetrate into the rear of Singapore town. Mike Blackwood, with an anti-tank weapon and only one or two men, took up positions at the roadblock and engaged the leading tank at point-blank range.

He gained precious time for defenders back in the heart of Singapore.

The brigadier himself was known to those of us who had long service records in India as a fine soldier.

He was a powerfully built, handsome officer, his face deeply tanned from years of service, his iron-grey moustache always neatly clipped, his eyes shrewd and quizzical.

Always a great all-round athlete of exceptional strength, he took tremendous pride in his physical fitness, and on numerous occasions was able to outmarch men many years his junior.

On the *Rooseboom*'s third evening out from Padang, Brigadier Paris invited a number of officers to have a drink with him. He gave what he called 'the obvious toast': safe arrival in Colombo.

'Forty-eight hours more should find us in happier and more comfortable circumstances,' he said.

But five hours later, just ten minutes short of midnight, the torpedo struck.

I had fallen asleep on a mattress on the deck, beside Willie MacDonald. I woke to find myself lying sprawled in the scuppers, half through the rails.

There was a weight pressing on my face and chest. As I pushed it off, I realised that it was all that was left of MacDonald.

Around me was indescribable noise. Screams, shouts, groans, the noise of escaping steam and inrushing water but above all, the bellowing of a bullock which we had taken on as rations.

I staggered along the deck which was already sloping steeply. The port boats, I saw, had been destroyed.

The captain and crew were attempting to lower one of the two boats on the starboard side. Around the other was a milling crowd and as I watched, something broke and the boat crashed bow-first into the sea, catapulting dozens of people with it.

I ran to the side. Oddly enough I felt no pain, though I was to find out later that my collarbone was broken, a piece of metal had lodged in my shin and my eardrum had burst from the blast.

The deck rail was almost awash. As I threw myself into the water and came to the surface, the one thing I remained conscious of was the continuing noise.

The predominant sound of the bullock's frenzied bellowing had given way to a high-pitched, monotonous wail from some native seaman somewhere out in the darkness.

Voices were shouting, 'Where are you, Mac?', 'Is that you, Jock?' There were choking cries for help.

Somewhere to my left, a soldier's voice inevitably started singing 'Roll out the Barrel'. Near me a naked man clung to a piece of floating debris. I swam towards him and shouted, 'Do you mind if I share your piece of wood?'

'By all means, old man,' he replied.

He was Assistant Commissioner Roger Owen Davis of the Malay Police. Assistant Commissioner Davis was the son of the Reverend Gerald Davis, Rector of Sturminster Marshal, at Wimborne, Dorset. Since my return to Britain I have learned more about him. He had been intended for the R.A.F. but a defect was discovered in his eyesight, and he was transferred to the colonial service. He was an exceptionally good Chinese scholar, and much of his work lay in following up on Communist and Japanese spies in the Malay States. The Japanese marked him down as 'a dangerous person', and in 1937 he was decorated by the King for gallantry in a clash with bandits. He had a chance to escape from Singapore to Australia, but was anxious to continue his war service in India and the Far East. His wife and son reached Durban safely. He was to live only twenty-four hours in the lifeboat. He was to slump down exhausted on the evening of the first day, and be crushed to death in the night.

Davis and I must have clung for an hour to the piece of wood before we saw, some distance away and shadowy in the moonlight, the blurred figures of people standing up in a lifeboat.

We kicked out and slowly made our way towards it. The scene was pandemonium. The boat had been damaged as they had launched her, and there was a gaping hole in her port bow.

Men scrambling aboard her forced the hole below water so that she filled almost to the gunwales.

As we arrived, the Dutch captain and his officers were shouting to the crowd about them to give them a chance to get her repaired.

We stayed there, dozens of us treading water while they plugged the hole with shirts, socks, singlets and shorts. Then a R.A.O.C. man climbed in and patched over the hole with a piece of tin.

A shout came from the captain: 'Any women and children out there?'

Yes, there were three women, no children.

'Any wounded?'

Yes, four or five of them.

Then, one by one, we were pulled aboard. It was only when someone seized my arm and a sharp pain shot through my shoulder that I cried out, 'By God, I'm wounded too!'

Numbly, still dazed by what had gone before, we waited for

the dawn.

The boat was so crowded. As I have said, it was built to hold twenty-eight people not the eighty who now occupied it. Most of us were standing shoulder to shoulder, face to face or back to back. It was impossible to change position.

As dawn crept up and lit the scene, we saw others who were dependent on the boat—some fifty of them clinging to the lifelines on the sides.

Around us, within a radius of half a mile, were the bobbing heads of still more survivors.

The boat itself was down nearly to the gunwales in the water.

I looked around for familiar faces.

I was in the stern. I could see Brigadier Paris. He was wearing only a khaki shirt, the pliers-and-hammer badge of the R.A.O.C. on its arm. A warrant officer had handed the shirt to him as he had climbed naked into the boat.

Close by, his hand on the tiller, was the stout red-faced captain of the *Rooseboom*.

He was wearing a white shirt and trousers with his epaulettes still in evidence. He, his chief officer and chief engineer—both Dutchmen like him—were the only men in the boat who were really adequately covered.

I, for instance, was still wearing the khaki shorts in which I had been sleeping when the torpedo struck.

There were three women in a group in the stern.

One I recognised as Mrs Gertrude Nunn, wife of Mr R. L. Nunn who had been Director of Works in Singapore. She was pleasant-faced and motherly looking, dressed in a khaki shirt and slacks.

There was a large, stout, fair-haired woman of thirty or so, dressed in a blouse and skirt and carrying a handbag. She was the wife of Dirk, the Dutch chief officer.

The third was a slim, pretty Chinese girl, clad in a coloured skirt and shirt, her feet bare.

Perched up in the bows, beyond a packed group of white men (mostly soldiers), I could see a group of about a dozen Javanese seamen. In their midst was their *serang*, or bosun. He was a white-haired old fellow with a fringed beard. A kind-looking man.

3

We welcomed the first dawn. There was, indeed, one wild delirious moment when we imagined that the morning star was the light of a ship coming over the horizon.

But in the days which followed, how we were to curse and hate that brassy, blazing, burning horror: the sun.

It was the sun which, more than any other factor, drove our fellows to crazed, demoniac acts and ends. It branded unbearable wounds on our unprotected bodies and scorched out of us the moisture that was life.

On the first morning, however, the sun was merely light and heat after a shivering, shock-shattering night. For one thing, it let us take stock of our position. It let us see how unbelievably crowded our human cargo really was.

We were standing so close that, night after night that followed, no man could lie down to sleep. He had to doze upright, his head leaning on the shoulder or breast of his opposite number.

To slump down was to risk being pressed into the bilge water which was always lapping in the bottom of the boat and there, to suffocate or drown.

A count revealed that our company numbered 135 in all, including the people around us in the water.

Certainly within an hour or two the number was less. Already there were some who could hold on no longer, who just loosened their grasp and drifted away.

We took a tally of our food and water. With sinking hearts we heard the total announced.

There was a case of bully beef, containing forty-eight 12-ounce tins. There were two 7-pound tins of fried spiced rice which the Dutch call *nasi goreng*. We had forty-eight tins of Colombo condensed milk and six Bols gin bottles full of fresh water.

Some of the soldiers had their water bottles, but nearly all had filled with salt water during the hours in the sea.

The Dutch captain regarded the meagre store bitterly. He had stocked this boat carefully with food, water, emergency gear and medical kit. In the mad scramble in the darkness, when the boat had all but foundered, almost everything had floated away into the night.

Brigadier Paris stood up in the stern sheets and called for attention.

He was probably more exhausted at that moment than anyone in the boat, for he had been drawn down with the *Rooseboom* as she sank, and he had come to the surface—'God knows how,' he said—with bursting lungs and a stomach full of water.

Now he stood there, very erect, legs bare beneath his shirttail, and addressed his troops as if on a parade ground.

'The captain,' he said, 'will be in command of the boat. I shall be responsible for discipline.

'We were due in Colombo at dawn on Tuesday. This is Monday. When we don't turn up by Thursday they are bound to send something out to look for us. That being so, the captain has decided that it will be wiser to stay here, in the vicinity of the sinking. Something should reach us by Friday.

'Our position is pretty sticky. But I look to you all, as British soldiers, as men who have acquitted themselves well on the peninsula, to retain your soldierly qualities until help arrives.'

He told us that we would receive a tablespoonful of water at each sunrise and a spoonful of milk and water at night.

A tin of bully beef would be shared between twelve people each day. From her handbag the Dutch mate's wife produced, of all surprising things, a tablespoon, which was to act as our measure for all the time our water lasted.

She was carrying, too, some thirst-quenching tablets which she shared. It was the sort of gesture which gladdened our first hours.

Later she showed some of us her useless Dutch banknotes, thousands of guilders which formed the greater part of the rest of her handbag's contents.

Officers to whom the brigadier could delegate some of his

responsibilities included: the two lieutenant colonels, J. P. Acworth of the Indian Army and R. E. Palmer of the Royal Engineers; and two majors, Richard Dent of the Indian Army and Noel Corrie of the Engineers.

Acworth swiftly showed himself a strong character. He was a cleanly built, balding man of forty-five or so with a striking guardee moustache.

He took charge of the rationing and announced that, to lessen the rigours of overcrowding, every man who was not injured had to take a compulsory spell of four hours each day clinging to the lifelines in the water.

The brigadier himself took one of the first spells in the water. While he was there, two sharks made their appearance—the first of many that we saw at various stages—but we yelled and beat at the water to drive them off.

During one of the spells in the water, a young soldier was stung by some kind of fish and pulled aboard in great agony. He died an hour later.

Towards the evening of the first day, there was a dramatic arrival on our boat.

We were joined by Lieutenant-Colonel Douglas of the Indian Army Ordnance Corps who had swum from a raft some hundred yards away. We could see that his nerves were strung to breaking point.

He told us that with him on the raft had been a white woman, her leg blown off by the explosion, a lance corporal of the Argylls (from whose description I at once recognised to be Jock Gray, one of the men who had trekked with me through the jungle after the Battle of Slim River) and Major Angus MacDonald, the brigade major I have mentioned before. Seven years later I gave evidence in the court action in Edinburgh which decided that Major MacDonald had to be dead.

Douglas said that MacDonald took with him from the ship a flask which he thought contained water. It was actually brandy and MacDonald had spent the day on the raft drinking it in an attempt to assuage his thirst.

The effects in the heat had been disastrous.

'Angus MacDonald is raving mad,' said Douglas. 'I had to leave him. He was trying to push me off the raft.'

We gave Douglas a spoonful of milk and water. Vaguely—for there were so many other things to occupy my attention—I could hear his voice rising excitedly as he continued his tale.

As darkness fell, the voice rose to a shout. Douglas would speak one sentence in English, the next in Urdu. It was a crazy, high-pitched babble.

Suddenly there was the noise of a scrimmage. He had struck out at all around him. I heard voices say, 'Put him over before he tips the boat up.'

There was a splash.

Colonel Douglas struggled to the side and gripped the gunwale. Someone fended him off with an oar. He slipped back into the darkness, shouting a crazy stream of Urdu curses.

Early next morning, the man I have always thought was the bravest of all amongst us stepped forward with a suggestion. It was Major Noel Corrie.

It would ease the well-nigh unbearable overcrowding, he told the brigadier, if he and some volunteers could construct a raft on which they might be towed behind the drifting boat.

Corrie and about twenty of the men, including two or three of the Javanese seamen, swam around collecting debris with which to construct their raft.

When they had completed it, it was a shaky structure, twenty feet by twenty feet, tied together with pieces of cord, strips of cloth and sisal fibre they'd salvaged from the sea.

They used the sisal to also make a towrope which they attached to the stern of the boat. Then the twenty of them climbed aboard, and the raft sank until they were waist deep in water.

Corrie must have known that there could be only one end to the course he had taken.

Man after man, through the three days that followed, members of his little band slipped off and disappeared. At last there was only Corrie himself, dazed with exhaustion, his upper body blackened by the sun, his legs bleached by the water.

Numbers in the boat had dwindled and the brigadier ordered Corrie to return.

He was pulled aboard, more dead than alive, and his gallant, piteous little craft was cut adrift.

He died that night.

Meantime the three women had drawn together. There they were, three of their sex in a cramped, sweating, groaning congregation of men: the Jocks, the Cockneys and the lascar seamen.

Already little codes of behaviour had materialised. A small space had been cleared so that the women could recline against the thwarts, half-sitting, half-lying.

When needs of the toilet had to be attended to, the brigadier would give the order, 'Everyone look to the bows,' and we would gaze ahead and give the women their spell of privacy.

Now that there was room to move, with men doing their four hours in the water and others on the raft, Mrs Nunn went among the wounded, tending to their injuries.

Her husband had died as he pushed her to safety. Dry-eyed and with pride she told me the story as she tied my arm behind me in a rough rope sling, seeking to alleviate the grating pain of my broken clavicle.

They had been in their cabin when the torpedo struck. Within seconds, water began to pour across the floor.

Mr Nunn lifted his wife and pushed her through the porthole.

It was one of those wide, square portholes typical of that type of Dutch coaster.

She came to the surface. He did not follow.

They had been a devoted couple. Friends have since told me many stories which help to explain the inspirational influence of Mrs Nunn in the lifeboat.

Before her marriage, as Gertrude Higgs, she was a celebrated contralto singer. She sang at the Promenade concerts with the Royal Choral Society, and at many other big concerts in Britain and abroad.

Her husband, in addition to being Director of Public Works in Singapore, was a group captain in the volunteer air service.

He had served as a civil engineer in Trinidad, Nigeria and British Guiana, and so rapid had been his rise through the ranks that he had been expected to become a colonial governor.

They had been on holiday in England when war was declared. Mr Nunn was recalled to Singapore. His wife, whose loyalty and devotion were a byword among their friends, flew out to be with him.

They left Singapore a day before it fell but their ship, the *Kuala*, was bombed and sunk before it had gone very far.

Mr Oswald Gilmour, who was Deputy Municipal Engineer in Singapore, told how Mrs Nunn then refused to leave her husband.

Survivors from the *Kuala* struggled to reach the island of

Pohm-Pohm, where Mr Nunn took charge.

He arranged the order of rescue: first women, children and wounded, then civilians, then Singapore's Public Works Department Unit and last the Services and himself.

A launch arrived and set about taking off as many as it could.

Some women with hospital experience volunteered to stay behind and look after the wounded who were left.

'Mrs Nunn,' says Mr Gilmour, 'got down as far as the embarkation spot, and then asked me to find her husband for her. He came along and she said to him, "Rex, I don't want to go if you are not coming." She evidently persuaded him to allow her to stay, for she did not leave the island until she was able to accompany him.'

When the final batch of survivors was taken from the island by junk and motor launch, Mr and Mrs Nunn were the last to go. They were brought to Padang and the *Rooseboom*.

The name of the Chinese girl who sat with Mrs Nunn and the Dutch mate's wife was, I learned, Doris Lim.

She spoke English with a marked American accent, a relic of the American convent in Shanghai whose sisters had brought her up.

She had worked for British Intelligence in Northern China. She had escaped from Tientsin just before the Japanese occupation there. She was again just a jump ahead of them out of Shanghai and then Hong Kong.

In Singapore, she had taken a post as assistant to a Chinese news cameraman.

Her experiences in the escape from Singapore were very similar to those of Mrs Nunn. The ship in which she was evacuated was bombed and sunk just a couple of miles from the spot where the Nunns' ship also went down.

Doris was the only woman among the passengers who escaped to an island from which she, in turn, was brought on to Padang and the *Rooseboom*.

As she sat there in the lifeboat, she looked very young and very pretty, even by European standards. Her complexion was particularly noticeable as it had a fresh bloom to it, unusual in a Chinese girl.

During the early days in the boat, she hardly spoke at all. She would sit gazing ahead of her with the unsmiling stoicism of her race.

And perhaps it was that fatalism, that refusal to be stampeded into despair, which led to our staggering ashore, she and I, on our island a thousand miles away.

4

On that first morning we took a count and found that there were 135 of us. At least half our number were raw young troops of the 18th Division, just out from home.

They were the boys who had been sent in a last-minute bid to bolster up the crumbling Malayan defences, but who had been diverted when it was seen that the fall of Singapore was inevitable.

They were all conscripts, nineteen and twenty years old with no experience in India. There must have been seventy of them. They were the first to crack, which was only natural. They sat silent, motionless, despondent.

We 'old sweats' wisecracked and kidded them in an attempt to put heart into them.

'Cheer up, sonnie,' we would say. 'It won't be long now. Just keep thinking about that beer in Colombo.'

We kept making them go over the side for a swim. We felt this was terribly important. It would keep them cooler and take their minds off things.

All the soldiers doing their compulsory four-hour spells clinging to the lifeline in the water had to take turns by night as well as by day.

Mrs Nunn had become our Florence Nightingale, our Mother Superior. She was always making her way around the lifeboat, trying to cheer up the unhappy boys.

Their conversation with her was always the same. 'Do you think anything will come? It isn't hopeless, is it? We're bound to be rescued, aren't we?'

And Mrs Nunn would always reply, 'Of course, don't doubt it. The one important thing is that we should keep a grip on ourselves.'

There was one boy who impressed me greatly at this time, a young C.Q.M.S. (from Ordnance or Engineers, I cannot recall which). He was only about twenty-one but he had about him a timbre and a toughness that was lacking in the others. I kept thinking what a regular he would have made.

He would speak to me about his girl. 'She's a lovely thing,' he would say. 'I wonder if they've told her by now. She'll be wondering what's happened to me!'

'She won't have to wonder long,' I would reply. 'Send her a cable from Colombo.'

There were plenty of us who were still cheerful and optimistic in spite of the fact that, from the second day on, hunger, thirst and the cramped quarters began to tell.

The thirst was worse than the hunger.

Hunger's gnawing pain seemed to reach a climax fairly soon and then we forgot about it.

But thirst—I was always thirsty. For a day or two one could make saliva, but afterwards one's throat was always as dry as a board. One always seemed to be trying to swallow, always licking one's lips, and with each day the effort to do so became more painful.

I was more fortunate than most in that the sun did not bother me. This was partly because of my years in India when I had often worn nothing but shorts, and partly because of my black Highlander's colouring and consequent pigmentation.

Others began to blister from the first day. It was the fair-haired Dutchmen who suffered the most. People began to tear off what little clothes they had so that they might dip them in the salt water and place them on their heads.

Yet even this seemed to be a mistake, for the salt water would run down the blistered skin of their faces and make the pain worse than before.

The Dutch captain picked up his sodden, useless charts and used them as a head covering. Doris Lim and Mrs Nunn used their shirts, sitting naked from the waist up.

All of us, at various stages in that first week, became prey to hallucination.

The first victim was a most unlikely one. He was a colour

sergeant of the Gordon Highlanders, a little dried-up nut of a man who had served for fifteen or sixteen years in the Far East, and who was known as 'Tich' to all of us.

One morning he said, 'It won't be long now till the flying boat gets back.'

'What flying boat?' I asked him.

'The one that came last night,' he said and I felt my heart jump in hope.

Then he continued. 'The one that took the women and wounded off.'

Looking towards the stern I saw the Dutchwoman, Mrs Nunn and the Chinese girl lying back against the thwarts and knew that Tich had been the first of us to see a mirage.

Almost all of us, at some stage, would imagine we saw a ship.

Once, a soldier leaned over the side of the lifeboat and drank from the sea.

'It's fresh,' he cried. 'The water's fresh.'

It shows our state of mental receptiveness because we struggled over to join him, wildly believing that what he said was true.

Some, indeed further gone than others, drank and said, 'He's right. It is fresh.'

We had begun to dream—fierce, vivid dreams of food, drink and friendly gatherings. We would later compare these dreams, and nearly all of them had the same points in common.

Then we would wake to the creak, creak, creak of the dried timbers as the boat swayed in the current.

For years afterwards—in the Jap prison camp, back in Singapore, London or Scotland—I could not rid myself of the fearsome feeling that my life was just another dream, and I would wake again to that creaking sway.

Almost everyone was experimenting with the drinking of sea water.

At first, when the youngsters were detected scooping it up in their hands from over the side, we tried to stop them.

Acworth, still the strongest character, made it an order that they must not drink from the sea.

But during the night there was much surreptitious drinking, and gradually people ceased to care. The effect on those who drank large quantities was to send them into a coma from which they never emerged, except crazed and suicidal.

Those who drank sea water in tiny quantities, however, seemed to suffer no really bad effects. From the beginning I myself gargled with the salt water and cleaned my teeth with it.

At the end of the first week I started to drink sea water in very small quantities, just a tiny scoopful in my hands when the thirst became unbearable.

Yet I found the best relief for my parched throat came from gargling the water without swallowing it and somehow, through the days that followed, it became a fetish with me to perform these tasks of cleaning my throat and teeth with regularity.

Almost up to the end, just as long as I had strength to lift my arms and rub my fingers over my teeth, I maintained the ritual.

It was on the third day that people were first detected drinking their urine. Some youngster started it and, turning to his mate, said, 'It's okay.'

It became imitative. I did it myself. At first the taste was nauseating, but then someone suggested that we mix the urine with salt water. We did so and it didn't seem so bad.

Later, the taste became so acidic that one felt as if one were drinking petrol. I quickly gave it up.

Slowly the spirit of comradeship with which we had set off began to vanish. We found ourselves watching our fellows covertly, suspiciously.

From the beginning there had been a careful watch on the rations. 'But who,' we began to think, 'is watching the watchers?'

Some of us became particularly watchful of a group from another regiment, five of them, who sat huddled together up near the bows, talking in undertones and looking round furtively at the other occupants of the boat.

There had been some suggestion early on that they were deserters. They had been stationed somewhere on some island near Singapore. Before the *Rooseboom* sailed they had been heard to speak of the possibility of getting a small boat and sailing over to Dutch territory together.

Now, as they sat there, all small men, all malevolent, keeping themselves to themselves and greeting all approaches from others with some obscene rejoinder, one sensed that they were up to no good.

Many of us had already gone. One of the first was Major Richard Dent, 'Dicky' to everyone.

On the first day, as he did his four-hour spell in the water, he grinned up to us and said, 'It's just like a Mediterranean cruise, isn't it?'

But he was one of those officers—and there are many of them in India—who never expose their bodies to the sun. Now he was among the first to suffer the worst agonies of sunburn.

He just vanished in the night.

We saw another indication of how things were going when a sergeant major, who had been given a life belt for his spell in the water because he could not swim, refused to come back to the boat to hand it over to another non-swimmer.

He clung to the life belt as if it was his last link with this world. Officers ordered him to hand it over, and in the end it was forcibly taken off him.

That night we could hear his voice raised in the darkness as he proclaimed his grievance. We heard someone strike him. Next morning, he had gone.

That was the way it was happening. People just disappeared in the night, and we met their departure with a dull acceptance. No one asked any questions.

At the back of our minds, already beginning to work to the theme of 'If it's not the other fellow, it'll be me', was the feeling that every man fewer meant more room in the boat.

The third night saw the biggest cut in our numbers so far. A storm blew up, the sea was very high and we shipped a lot of water. We baled frantically with such utensils as we had, but there were many who panicked.

Out of the night we heard the sound of screams and shouts, and in the morning twenty people were missing.

I think it was then that we really began to realise what the five men in the bows were up to.

They had formed themselves into a murder gang, determined that, if everyone else had to go, they would still live.

Next morning rations were cut. A tin of bully beef was now shared between twenty people. The two spoonfuls of water per day became one.

Each day's hand-outs became an ordeal. It was like feeding a band of ravenous wild animals.

Acworth had ordered that the rations be brought up to the stern where officers were positioned so that we might watch them ourselves. All eyes centred on us, hour after hour. We evolved a system to see that no man tried to come back a second time for a share.

Acworth stood in the stern pouring the precious drops of water into the spoon. Men would cry out, 'You haven't filled the spoon. I haven't had a full share.'

Acworth ordered me to stand beside him, checking the faces of the men as they drew their rations.

If I said that a man had already had his spoonful, Acworth was adamant in his refusal to give him any more. Many cursed him and screamed that they had had none.

The Javanese were the calmest at such moments. For the first day or two, they had refused to take any water. We had to say to them, 'Come along there, you've got to have it.'

It was as if they sensed the feeling against them which existed among some of the men. (There *was* a faction which said, 'To hell with the blacks. Why should we suffer for them?')

That mood changed swiftly when the men began to look to the Javanese as their main hope of salvation.

We, too, were bearded and black. It was hard to say who was the white man and who was the Javanese.

The sun seemed to beat down more fiercely than ever on the brassy ocean.

For two days the blond first officer had been lying in a coma, his head in his wife's lap, his face burned, blistered and swollen to unrecognisable shape. She sat, speaking to no one else, crooning

Dutch words of comfort to him.

On the fourth night we heard him utter a stream of Dutch sentences. We heard her say, '*Nae, nae,*' as she sought to dissuade him. He had told her that he was going for help.

Suddenly he broke away from her and shouted to us in English, 'Going ... going to swim ... find help.' Then he sprang over the side and swam away into the darkness, quite calmly and with some unsuspected reserve of strength.

His wife did not weep. She sat for nearly another day in an attitude of resignation, keening and moaning softly to herself. At sunset there was a movement in the boat and she was overboard.

I was standing beside one of the lascars as it happened. I watched her drift away and I felt that I *could* go after her, that I *should* go after her. But I did not go.

That was how it was, with me as with everyone else. We were beginning to find out how little man-made codes count when man is facing the ultimate.

One incident about this time tore me with an anguish of a kind I thought I had ceased to be capable of.

A soldier I had known for years—a fine fellow, a Scotsman, one of our best athletes and most uncomplaining soldiers—went overboard for a swim to freshen himself up.

He allowed himself to get just a fraction too far out of range of the drifting boat. He found he was not catching up with it when he tried to return.

He was swimming with an overarm trudgen stroke and I saw him change to breaststroke.

Slowly he fell further away from us as his stroke weakened. We lay, even those of us who watched him, too spent to think of any measure which might aid him.

Finally, as his face emerged from the water at the end of a stroke, I saw his expression of determination change to an unforgettable one of utter despair.

I saw him realise that he was going to drown.

I watched his bobbing head until it must have been 200 yards away, with nothing all around it but the sea.

It was half an hour before a big wave hid him from view and when we looked again, he was not there.

5

AS the first week drew to its close, Brigadier Paris sank back into a torpor, speaking to no one, getting weaker with every hour.

After the effort of his speech to the troops, made soon after he had fought his way to the surface, he had said little. Lieutenant-Colonel Acworth had been the directing force.

But the brigadier had a guardian.

He was Mike Blackwood, the young officer who had sailed him out of Singapore in his yacht.

Captain Mike Blackwood had joined us on the afternoon of the second day. He had been swimming about from the time the ship sank.

Because he was red-haired and had that freckled pigmentation which cannot take the sun, his face and shoulders were a raw mass. The lower part of his body was bleached by the water so it was a strange blue colour.

But his good spirits were astounding.

Soon after coming aboard he said, 'I am afraid it's up to you and me, Gibson, to look after the brigadier.'

I had known him well in India. In the summer of 1939,

just before the brigadier's departure to Malaya, there had been a training course designed to find men 'capable of commanding a company on active service'. Mike Blackwood, not long out of Sandhurst, finished top. I, then a lance corporal, finished third.

Now, with almost unbelievable fortitude—for the pain of his sunburn must have been worse than anyone's—Blackwood performed little duties for the rapidly weakening Paris, even to the extent of saving part of his tiny water ration for him.

It was a shock when the brigadier suddenly raised his head and, turning to Blackwood, said quite lucidly, quite quietly and very pleasantly, 'I say, let's go along to the club for a drink.'

Blackwood answered him as conversationally as if they had been strolling down St James's. 'Let's make it later, sir,' he said.

Within an hour the brigadier was thrashing violently about the boat, his mind completely gone, while Blackwood and I sought to hold him down.

By morning, which was the Friday on which he had had hopes of rescue from Colombo, Brigadier Paris was in a final coma. Brigadier A. C. M. Paris was the son of one soldier (Major-General Sir Archibald Paris, K.C.B.) and the father of another (a major in the Royal Signals). He himself joined the Oxfordshire and Buckinghamshire Light Infantry from Sandhurst in 1909. His brigade, the Secunderabad Light Infantry Brigade, was sent to Singapore in July 1939.

Brigadier Paris took over command of the 11th Division in

Malaya on 23 December 1941, and held the frontal Japanese advance for several days. When Singapore fell he was ordered, as a jungle warfare expert, to embark for India. He reached Sumatra five days before the sinking of the *Rooseboom*.

Mike Blackwood announced his death to the troops. Men stood silent as we slipped him over the side, and Blackwood repeated such passages of the burial service as he could remember.

The brigadier was the only one, of all those whose lives ended there, for whom we could summon the strength to have such a service.

Poor Mike Blackwood survived his friend by only a day. He slipped unconscious to the bottom of the boat, and we found him drowned in the lapping six inches of bilge water. Captain Mike Blackwood was twenty-three years old. He had a family example of service and self-sacrifice before him. An ancestor commanded the frigate *Penelope* at Trafalgar. His father, Colonel F. H. Blackwood of the Lincolns, was a D.S.O. during the 1914–1918 war. As a small boy he saw his father drowned in British Guiana, trying to save a girl bather who was in difficulties.

Michael went from Wellington College to Sandhurst in 1936. He was a great games player and keen horseman. It was while he was a cadet at the Royal Military College that he developed the love of yachting which led him to sail Brigadier Paris to Sumatra when Singapore fell. He joined the Argylls in 1937, and went out to India at the time of Munich.

Earlier in the night he did a very typical thing.

He turned to me and said, 'I should not have told you, Gibson, but in the circumstances I feel it is in order to mention it, now that it can't make any difference to either of us. The brigadier had recommended you for the D.C.M.'

Mike had been in charge of records, and I can imagine the conflict in his mind as he lay beside me in the boat. Should he do that unforgivable thing from a regular soldier's point of view and reveal a confidence? Or should he speak a heartening sentence to a man with perhaps only a few hours to live?

Within two hours of the brigadier's funeral, the Dutch captain was stabbed by one of his own engineer officers.

The old man was dozing, his hand still on the tiller, when we heard a shout, a sudden splutter of Dutch invective. Before anyone could get to him, the engineer had jumped at the skipper and buried a knife in his ribs.

Apparently he had been sitting nursing a grievance, blaming the skipper for our troubles. No one even knew he had a knife in his belt.

'Grab him,' shouted Acworth, and someone flung himself on the engineer as he tried to snatch the few remaining rations.

That was the strange feature of every suicide. As people decided to jump overboard, they seemed to resent the fact that others were being left with a chance of survival.

They would try to seize the rations and fling them overboard. They would try to make their last action in the boat the pulling of the bung which would let in the water.

Their madness always seemed to take the form that they must not go alone but must take everyone with them.

The engineer who had stabbed the captain failed to get to the rations but tore himself loose and jumped overboard.

He, too, was still strong enough to swim away, and I have since reflected that all the Dutchmen, except the murdered captain, went swimming off: the mate, his wife, the engineers.

Mrs Nunn bathed the captain's wound with salt water. He just lay there saying in English, 'Finished, finished, finished ... it is the finish.' Then he would murmur the same thing in his own tongue: '*Kaput ... kaput ...*' Every now and again we caught the English word, 'finished'.

He died that night, his head in Mrs Nunn's lap.

I was now guard of the water bottles. There were only two left, and one of them only half full.

I dozed with them under my body. In the night I was awakened by a shout, and then the voice of Mrs Nunn. 'He's trying to steal the water.'

There was a hand feeling under me. I grabbed.

It was the chief engineer, the sole surviving Dutchman. Crying something angrily in Dutch, he flung himself into the water.

Strangely it was now that the Javanese, who hitherto had seemed afraid of the soldiers, assumed a new manner.

It was as if they knew that they, the only seamen left aboard, were now superior to the landsmen.

Their manner took on a subtle difference.

The *serang* came up to the stern and took over the tiller.

None of the white men did anything to resist this assumption of authority. Rather, indeed, we encouraged it.

Our manner changed, too. We became subservient to the Javanese.

They took it in turns to manage the rudder, and we found ourselves consulting them.

'Are we far from land, *serang*?' we would ask. And always his reply was the same: '*Tedah tao.*' ('I don't know.')

Every evening someone would imagine he saw land. 'Is that not land, *serang*?' we would shout.

On the seventh evening, the Sunday, we finished the last bottle of water.

Palmer was in command now, but for all the effort that he could muster, it was an empty title. He sat there, hunched up and weak, his face bird-like, the cheekbones standing out.

Then we saw Mrs Nunn talking with him, and Palmer roused himself to speak to the boat's company in a voice little above a whisper.

'I don't think there is much hope for us,' he said. 'I'm afraid we must reconcile ourselves to the fact that if something doesn't turn up pretty soon, it will be too late. Mrs Nunn has suggested that we commit ourselves to God. She would like to conduct a service.'

Somehow, heaven knows how, we had a Bible, water-logged and tattered. To whom it had belonged—Jock soldier from some Highland village, young public-school lieutenant or the convent-reared Chinese girl—I will never know.

Mrs Nunn stood up, her face blackened by the sun. Like the voices of us all by now, hers cracked and whispered through thirst and weakness.

She opened the Bible and began to read aloud.

We all seemed automatically to turn towards her. This strange, mixed bag of tortured, desperate human beings.

We sang with her 'Abide with Me' and 'The Lord is my Shepherd'. We said the Lord's Prayer.

Each and all of us felt almost physically drawn towards Mrs Nunn.

Months later I talked about it with a psychiatrist in the prison camp.

'You were all overcome,' he said, 'by that urge which seizes every man in time of danger—the urge to return to the safety of the womb. To all of you, Mrs Nunn personified the mother.'

This story, I know, must now be impressing as nothing but one of unrelieved tragedy. A chronicle of hours in which the only milestones seem to be the deaths of men or women.

But that was how it was.

There were perhaps fifty or sixty of us left when the service was held. Thereafter, men went quickly. Palmer ... Acworth ...

Colonel Acworth*, like so many, just vanished in the night. The calmness and efficiency with which he had sought to maintain discipline and morale in the boat were typical of him. Lieutenant-Colonel J. Pelham Acworth had been in the Indian Army since 1916. He served in France in the 1914–18 war and took part in a Frontier campaign with the Poona Horse. Later, he joined the Frontier Force, 4/12th. In 1932, when the 4/12th were Indianised and officers were given the chance to transfer to other units in case they had views on the colour question, Acworth stayed on. Much of his service was on the Staff in India. He met his wife while he was one of the Indian Army Instructors at Sandhurst in 1929. His son (for whom an Army career is planned) was born while he was at the Staff College at Quetta in 1933.

The 'supplies' role he had adopted in rationing out the food and water had come naturally to him, for he was A.A.Q.M.G. to the 11th Indian Division when Japan entered the war.

It was grimly, during the Monday, the eighth day, that I realised that if any discipline was to be retained, I must be the one to maintain it.

Up in the bows, malignant and threatening, sat the five deserters.

Mrs Nunn died that day.

She knew that she was going to die. Towards the end she spoke in endearing terms of her husband.

'I'm glad,' she said, 'he went with the ship and did not have to suffer with us here.'

She just slipped quietly into unconsciousness while Doris Lim, naked now beside her, bathed her lips with salt water.

I knew the dreadful things that had been happening to others who had died, and whose bodies had remained in the boat. So I said to Doris Lim, 'Get her over the side, quickly.'

We slipped her over before the evil band in the bows knew that she had died.

It was just at about this stage that the murder gang—as I have always thought of them since—came out into the open.

While others watched, helpless and apathetic, they jumped from behind on the young C.Q.M.S. of the 18th Division who had so impressed me in the early days, and drew a jagged bully beef tin across his throat.

There was no doubt as to their intentions. They had, as we knew, tried to drink the blood of people who had died, and had found it impossible.

Now they were trying butchery.

The youngster tore himself free and staggered towards us for protection. He lay there dying, painfully and lingeringly.

I said, 'For God's sake, put him overboard.'

Warrant Officer MacKenzie of the Indian Army Ordnance Corps then came to me. 'Don't you realise what is happening?' he said. 'Don't you know that we are all going to be killed? Those men intend to commandeer the boat.'

I did not feel brave at that moment. But I pulled myself together and addressed the whole company in as strong a voice as I could muster. I told them what we suspected.

'You crowd,' I said, pointing to the five, 'are dumping people overboard for your own ends. Do you think you can get away with that?'

Their ringleader leaned forward aggressively. He was a small man, about my own height and not bad looking.

He had, I remember, a coarse Liverpool accent. One finds thousands of his type in the Army: cross-grained, tough and malcontent. When you are a drill instructor, you must break them before they break you.

'We'll bloody well put you over as well if you don't shut up,' he said.

I think I muttered something about us being in the majority. But I did shut up. I was scared. This was no barrack square. I did not know how many I could rely upon to back me up.

I waited. Next time MacKenzie came to me I said, 'It's them

or us. There's only five of them. How many men can we rely on if we try to rush them and put them overboard?'

MacKenzie moved about among the others and when darkness came down, he told me that he had a majority. There were twelve to fourteen men ready to deal with the murder gang.

It was the showdown. I thought to myself, 'Well, here it is.' I had seen so many go over and not come back. We moved down the boat, converging on the five men up near the bows.

They sensed, of course, what was on. It must have been obvious what our purpose was.

All this time, I remember, the Javanese sat placidly in their places. They, too, must have known what was afoot, but they remained blank-faced and phlegmatic.

The atmosphere was electric. One little tough shouted, 'Here they come,' and from behind him pulled out a bottle and held it by the neck.

Drummer F. Hardy of the Argylls—a little chap, no more than five feet three inches in height, who had been one of our heroes in the Malayan fighting—sprang forwards. The bottle crashed down on his head. Two of the murder gang grabbed him and pushed him overboard. Drummer Hardy, formerly batman to Brigadier I. MacA. Stewart, commanding officer of the Argylls, earned an undying place in the history of the Argylls, not only as the last man to cross the Johore causeway into Singapore after the retreat from Malaya, but by the manner in which he crossed it.

When recalling the history of the regiment, Brigadier Stewart said that Hardy was a man who would never run. Not when Jap planes came over or when a demolition party was hurrying to join the main body. 'Japs were only Japs, and it was undignified for an Argyll to take any notice of them.'

On the morning when 30,000 men crossed the causeway from lost Malaya into doomed Singapore, Hardy and the C.O. were the last to leave.

The battered remnants of the Argylls had held the final bridgehead. The Australian rearguard had crossed the causeway, then the Gordons. Steady and heads high, the Argylls followed to the strains of 'Hielan' Laddie' and 'A Hundred Pipers', played by their own two remaining pipers.

'The sappers,' says Brigadier Stewart, 'were waiting impatiently to set off their demolition of the causeway, and it was imperative that the last party should hurry over before the Japs came.

'I encouraged Drummer Hardy to run but as I have said, he would never run properly, not even on jungle paths when nobody was looking and certainly not when Japs were about.

'In this dramatic stage setting, almost alone on three-quarters of a mile of open causeway, in the clear light of a tropical dawn, with the Japs coming and with the defenders of Singapore looking on, he became mutinous at such an indignity.

'Nothing I said had any effect. He just walked slowly all the way over.'

Then we were at their throats. We struggled, stumbled and rolled, wrestling at the bottom of the boat.

We did not seem to put them overboard one by one so much as to rush them overboard in a body.

As they came to the surface, three got their hands to the gunwale and tried to drag themselves back.

It was a confusion of pleadings, curses and choking half-smothered obscenities.

Relentlessly we battered at their fingers with the rowlocks. We were down to the elemental now. We told ourselves a dozen times that night it was either them or us.

6

It is when death comes slowly and inevitably, when nervous tension cannot be sustained, that men crack.

Since the war there have been experiments on rafts and lifeboats to see how long men can last with bare means of sustenance.

But how can these experiments tell the full story when the men in the boats know that they are never in any real danger?

Doctors and officers will visit them at intervals to see how they are getting on; newspaper photographers will fly overhead; they have only to signal and they will be back on land sipping beef tea.

In the real, long, drawn-out emergency, with hopes of rescue growing fainter with each succeeding day, it is the mind which cracks before the body. The body can always summon a last flicker of energy. But it has to be dictated by a refusal to accept death, a determination not to die, a knowledge that one was not meant to end like this.

Through the years that have since passed, I have been asked hundreds of times—by fellow prisoners, by psychiatrists, by Jap interrogation officers, by friends at home—'Why is it, do you think, that you lived when every other white man died?'

Hundreds of times I have puzzled over the reasons in my own mind.

I feel that I started with advantages over most of the other soldiers in the boat.

I had been a regular on foreign service for thirteen years. I was toughened to the climatic conditions of the East. I had served in some pretty hot places in India, particularly with Northern Command.

My broken collarbone had been a blessing in disguise. Because of it, Paris and Acworth told me that I did not have to do any spells in the water during those early, overcrowded days.

There is no doubt that the four hours a day clinging to the lifelines tolled heavily on the reserves of strength of all who did it. I escaped it.

Perhaps because long service had taught me a philosophy, I adopted a mood of passivity early on.

It seemed to me useless to butt in when so many were making plans and giving orders. I imagine that my quiescence had in it something parallel to the stoicism of Doris Lim, and that it served me in equal stead.

Also—and possibly this is the most important reason of all—I was determined not to die. It never crossed my mind that survival would come about because our boat would drift to land, but somehow I never had any doubt that we would be picked up.

Only very rarely did utter hopelessness descend on me.

And I do believe that it was the little matters of procedure, the adherence to my self-made rules about gargling, cleaning my teeth, etc., which served to maintain my morale. Once and once only did I surrender to the contagion of the suicidal urge.

It was by day that one felt the dreadful need to end it all.

Most of our suicides happened in daylight, when the sea was calm and warm, and one felt how easy it would be just to swim away into oblivion.

By night we cowered into the protection of the thwarts, afraid of the darkness and afraid of the sea.

One day, soon after the fracas with the murder gang, a youngster of the Loyal Regiment asked me if I thought there was a chance of any of us getting through our ordeal.

We debated the possibility of something turning up. Suddenly he said, 'I've had enough. I'm going to finish it. Will you come too?'

It was at a moment when I was feeling down. 'All right,' I said.

We decided that we would drink as much salt water as we could to make ourselves weak and ill, and then we would go over the side.

I drank until sheer sickness forced me to stop. Then we stood up, joined hands, took a deep breath and jumped together into the sea. We seemed to go down a fair way before I expelled the air from my lungs.

No sooner had I done so, and felt myself taking in sea water, than I was overcome by a desperate desire to get to the surface. 'I mustn't drown, I mustn't drown,' was the only thought in my mind as I tore my hand free from my companion's and kicked out.

When I came to the surface, the boat had drifted only three or four yards and I struck out madly to catch up with it. I pulled myself on board and lay there, panting and sick. As far as I know, the boy from the Loyals did not come to the surface again.

No one had paid the slightest attention to the incident. We were so far gone by then that no one interfered with each other's business in any way. Perhaps by this stage there was a score of us left. I cannot really say.

From then on it was just a case of another man fading out, and then the struggle, more and more difficult, to heave his body overboard. We had lost identity. Sun and salt water had rotted our remaining rags till we were all naked.

Great ulcerated sores, where the flesh just seemed to rot away and leave a hole big enough to take a man's fist, formed on all of us, particularly round the small of the back where we rubbed against the thwarts.

We had lost count of time, and the order in which incidents happened after the clash with the murder gang is hazy to me. But

I remember the day the rain came and the day, too, that we caught the gulls.

Many a time we had seen the rain far off in the distance. It would happen in the cold of the evening. We would see the rain moving across the horizon like a screen or curtain.

Tense and excited, we waited. 'It's coming, the rain's coming,' we said. Our mouths were open and our tongues out. And then we would see it move right away from us. Once or twice, indeed, it passed right over our heads.

Our rain, when it reached us, was a cloudburst, a three- or four-minute affair of huge, cold, battering drops which were nearly enough to make us forget our thirst and cower into the shelter of the boat.

As I was now in charge, I asked every man to control everything until we had filled the four empty Bols gin bottles which remained.

Everyone helped. No man tried to drink until, scooping with our hands, we had filled the bottles. The rainwater which collected in the bottom of the boat was, of course, mixed with the salt water already lapping there, but who cared about that? The bottles filled, we flung ourselves on hands and knees and lapped our fill while the rain lasted.

The gulls numbered about twelve. They were bigger than those you see around the British coast.

They arrived out of the blue, flew around the boat for some minutes and then settled, very tamely and seemingly with no fear at all of humans, on parts of the boat and on men's heads and shoulders.

We had gone tense and rigid. No man dared move. Then, with one accord, we pounced. We got seven of them!

Minutes later, there was nothing left but feathers settling around the boat. We tore the gulls to pieces and gulped the raw flesh.

And so it went on, hour after hour, day after day.

Drifting in a silence broken only by the creak of the timbers and the wash of the water. No man speaking, rarely moving. The Chinese girl and I sometimes clasped to each other for the comfort of animal warmth.

Only once throughout our whole time in the boat—and even then it was towards the end—did I think of Doris Lim with thoughts other than neuter.

Strangely in a man emaciated and spent as I was, I was suddenly seized with a male urge towards the girl as she lay in my arms. I began to fondle her.

She stared back at me with blank, lacklustre eyes. 'Please let me die in peace,' was all she said.

There was never such another moment between us.

There came a day—the most horrible of all in that odyssey

of horror—when a big gunner (whose name I never knew) and I gazed at each other and realised that we were the only two white men left aboard.

Wasted and skeleton-like though he was, he remained a man of fine physique. He was, I recall, very tall and very dark. A fine, wide-shouldered fellow. Without doubt he would have survived because a day later, God help us, we were to sight land.

But up in the bows sat the four Javanese who were still alive. The old *serang* was one of them. The girl and I were near the stern. The gunner lay on the starboard side, up nearer the bows. Suddenly I heard his voice say, 'Jock, Jock ... help me, Jock.'

We looked up and saw two of the Javanese pounding at the gunner's head with rowlocks. He had ceased to struggle. Blood was running from his head, down his shoulders and body.

As we watched, a third Javanese with a piece of tin which he had pressed to form a blade started tearing at the body of the gunner. I can still hear now, as we heard it then, the grating of the tin against bone and flesh.

The lascar plunged his hand into the wound, like someone groping in a handbag, and pulled out something dripping with blood into which he dug his teeth like a dog snatching at a bone. The other two ceased to hammer the gunner's head and grabbed greedily at the wound.

They were unquestionably mad. Blood dripped from their faces as, still chewing, they grinned horribly at us. One of them shouted at us and proffered something he held in his hands.

All we could do was shake our heads. This one vile meal seemed to be enough to satisfy them. As soon as it was over, they and the *serang* pushed the body overboard.

The *serang* died that night. We heard the other three chanting some kind of service in the dark. While they were about it, I crawled along the bottom of the boat and, one by one, found the rowlocks and threw them overboard. If we were to be the next to go, they must find some other weapon.

When daylight came, one of the Javanese made signs to indicate that they knew I had slipped the rowlocks into the water.

The girl and I dared not take our eyes off the three in the bow. We were determined that, at the slightest movement towards us, we would slip overboard together.

But at night we could not keep our eyes open. I woke with a jerk as I felt a movement near my elbow. It was one of the Javanese. He grinned his wolfish grin as he repeated a word over and over again. I did not understand but it was the Javanese word for 'land'.

He was pointing as he spoke and, looking over the side, I saw a shadow darker than the darkness. We clung, all five of us, to the edge of the boat, trying to drag ourselves up and peer into the night.

We had so often seen mirages that we were afraid to let ourselves believe that this was really land. So often what had looked like land had just dissolved into cloud. But this looked too big, too near, to be any cloud. I think all five of us—lascars, the girl, myself—heard it at the same time. It was an unmistakable sound.

It was the sound of surf breaking against coral.

Walter Gibson.

The 1,000-ton *Rooseboom*. She was carrying some 500 evacuees from Malaya to Ceylon when she was torpedoed. Only one of her lifeboats was launched.

TOP: Mr and Mrs R. L. Nunn—he died as he
pushed his wife to safety.
BELOW: Doris Lim (left), who survived with
Gibson; and Brigadier Paris (right), who was
responsible for discipline in the lifeboat.

Walter Gibson joined the Argyll and Sutherland
Highlanders at the age of fifteen and served in Asia for
seventeen years.

Captain Michael Blackwood—his fortitude was almost
unbelievable.

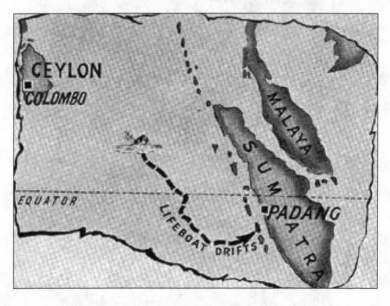

This sketch map shows the 1,000 miles the lifeboat drifted, from the spot where the Rooseboom sank to the island where Gibson crawled ashore.

Captain Ian Lapsley—the jungle and attrition claimed
a very brave officer.

Sergeant Willie MacDonald—his heart was in the
silver city that he was never to see again.

Doris Lim (left) and Janet Lim feeding the geese at the home of Doris's husband outside Padang in Japanese-occupied Sumatra, Indonesia. (©Janet Lim)

Japanese troops landing on Singapore island in 1942. (©National Archives of Singapore)

British prisoners of war marching on the road to Changi in 1942 during the Japanese Occupation.
(©National Archives of Singapore)

In Singapore General Itagaki, the Japanese commander in Malaya, signs the surrender of all Japanese forces in Southeast Asia. (©National Archives of Singapore)

7

All five of us were in tears, even the Javanese, as the noise of the surf grew louder and louder, and the shadow of the land larger and larger.

The speed of the boat's drift increased as we neared the shore. There was a jerk and a grating sound as she grounded. Then she swung round broadside, and the waves tilted her over.

We scrambled out and fell into the surf. The boat was aground on coral and the waves came crashing in, skittling us over as we tried to gain our feet.

I grabbed the girl's hand and together we crawled, staggered and fell towards the beach.

We could not speak but we made breathless, inarticulate grunting noises as we urged each other on.

Uppermost in my mind, as in hers she told me afterwards, was the prayer, 'Don't let us drown now, so close to safety.'

The coral tore our feet, knees and hands, but we were insensible to pain. We did not see the Javanese from the moment the boat grounded. Afterwards we found out that one of the three had drowned in the surf as he had tried to reach the beach.

On hands and knees we crawled over the last yards to dry

land. Together we lay there, gasping and exhausted.

I tried to stand up, but the whole place seemed to be swaying with the same motion as the boat. My first coherent thought was, 'Oh God, we've landed on a floating island. We're no better off. We shall just float here as we floated on the boat.'

We mumbled unintelligible nothings to each other. Hysterically we mouthed thanks for our deliverance. We kept trying to rise to our feet and collapsing again by the edge of the water. At last we managed to crawl a safe distance from the water and fell, clasped in each other's arms, into an exhausted sleep.

The island on which we had landed was Sipora, one of the Mentawai Islands which runs down a line sixty miles west of the coast of Sumatra. We had drifted over a thousand miles, and we must have been in the boat just one month.

The girl woke me. Something had disturbed her. All around us the beach was lit by glowing light which advanced and receded every few minutes. The air was filled with an incessant rustling noise, like the crumpling of paper.

As we lay still, the lights came nearer and the noise increased. It was an uncanny sensation. Then, as the light of dawn spread over the beach, we saw the explanation.

We were surrounded by huge crabs, hundreds of them, the size of dinner plates. The beach was literally covered with them. The glowing lights came from their eyes and the rustling noise was caused by their movement.

Above the beach lay a mangrove swamp. Beyond that, the jungle. We crawled to the swamp. We were so weak now that we could not even crawl on our hands and knees. Instead we pulled ourselves along on our bellies, dragging ourselves forwards using roots and bushes.

We lay in the swamp as the sun rose. The depression our bodies made in the mud quickly filled with black oily-looking water, which we lapped up in huge gulps.

It was the first large quantity of brine-free water we had tasted since the *Rooseboom* had sunk.

A great peace, a peace of utter exhaustion, fell upon us. I think we might have lain there and died had we not been spurred to further movement, first by leeches from the swamp and then by the flies, twice as large as British horseflies, which arrived to attack us. They drove us back to the beach.

Before we made the move, I should certainly have died but for Doris Lim.

I had fallen asleep again, and woke to find myself immersed in the swamp with only my head above the mud. The girl was supporting my shoulders and frantically urging me to shake myself free.

Oddly, from the time we reached land it was she who seemed to take the initiative. She who, from the first to the last day in the boat, had been completely passive.

Back on the beach, we looked out to where the lifeboat lay grounded on the coral. There was no sign anywhere of the Javanese. We must have lain on the beach for hours. Strange hallucinations seized me.

On the edge of the swamp, dead-looking leafless trees were growing. In their branches I could see the faces of person after person who had been in the boat. The wolf-like features of the Javanese, Mrs Nunn, Corrie and the brigadier were all there.

All the faces were immobile and stone-like. 'They have all got here,' I thought. 'They have petrified. That is what will happen to us.' Around me, on the rocks and stones on the beach, I saw other faces.

Suddenly I saw a figure skip down the beach into the sea and make towards the lifeboat. It was the figure of Piper McFayden who had been in the band of the Argylls in Secunderabad when I was also a piper. He had been no particular friend of mine, and I had not thought of him for years.

But there he was, dancing down the beach and striking out towards the lifeboat. I was seized by a choking, dreadful realisation that the lifeboat was evil, pure evil. I wanted to warn McFayden. I tried to shout to him, but no sound came out.

I can still remember clearly the effort I made to call the words, 'McFayden, keep away from that boat.' I watched him go right up to the boat and clamber in. Then the vision faded.

In moments of consciousness we could hear the birds whistling in the jungle behind us. We knew we should try to reach further inland and look for water, but we just had no strength left.

It must have been about midday when we saw, a hundred yards or so out to sea, a figure in a *sampan*. At first I thought it merely further hallucination, till I realised that Doris Lim had seen it too.

We watched as the *sampan* moved past the lifeboat and turned up the beach. This signified to me that over there must lie a creek of some kind.

We started to crawl towards it. It cannot have been more than 1,000 to 1,500 yards away, but it took us the whole of the afternoon and far into the night to cover the distance. We would advance a yard or two and then stop, exhausted.

At last, there before us in the moonlight were a sandbank and a wide stream. The beach sloped down to the water and together, we slithered down the decline.

We lay and gulped water. It was fresh. It seemed as if we would never stop drinking. We were too far gone to remember all the old precepts about sipping small quantities, but it seemed to do us no harm.

As fast as we drank, the water went through us, as if we were pouring it in at one end of a funnel only for it to run out of the other.

Replete, all our energy spent again, we scrambled from the

creek and fell asleep, huddled together behind a tree trunk on the beach.

We woke to find ourselves surrounded by a group of islanders.

They were fearsome enough figures. All were naked except for G-strings, and all were tattooed in blue from the naval to the lower lip.

They had no eyelashes, no eyebrows and their teeth were filed to a point. They carried spears, bows and machetes. They were Mentawais, a Polynesian tribe.

Thoughts flashed through my mind of *Robinson Crusoe*, cannibalism and cartoons of native stew pots. It sounds amusing enough now, but it was deadly serious then.

We pointed to our stomachs and to our mouths, but the figures just ignored us. They chattered among themselves, obviously discussing what they could do with us.

Then they turned and walked away up the creek towards the jungle. We could hear the thump of their drums and the sky was lit red by their fire.

About an hour or two later, a canoe appeared in the creek. It was paddled by two boys, about twelve or thirteen years old, carrying machetes.

They leaped ashore and came running towards us. Again we pointed to our mouths and stomachs.

They chattered and grinned that they understood. One of them ran to a coconut tree and brought back two green coconuts which they opened with their machetes. They watched us as we drank the juice and ate the pulp. Then they fetched others, cut them open, laid them beside us, returned to their canoe and paddled away.

At dawn there arrived another canoe with two people in it. They picked us up, placed us in their boat and paddled off into the open sea.

We must have travelled along the coast of the island for three or four hours before they turned into a beach, lifted us from the canoe and unceremoniously dumped us down.

We found out later that they had placed us where we would be found by members of a Malay village which was close by.

The island was used by the Dutch as a penal settlement, just as the Andaman Islands were used by India. The Malays were transportees who had formed a settlement close to the shore.

That evening, two Malays carried us, wrapped in *sarongs*, to their huts.

There, on a verandah, skeleton-like but alive, lay the two Javanese from the boat. They stared stonily at us, giving no greeting or sign of recognition.

We ravenously ate the fish and rice the Malays brought as our first meal. We stayed in that village for six weeks before the Japanese arrived and carted us off to a prison camp and a

new chapter. In that village we were to regain our flesh and our strength.

But one memory of the island stands out above all others.

It is of the day just after we landed when the Malays brought me a mirror.

I had grown used to the sight of the Chinese girl, her once-pretty features now the face of an old, old woman. It was a face framed in hair which was lank and matted. Her once-shapely body was now gaunt, emaciated and red raw where the boat had rubbed. Her ribs stood out and her dark, expressive eyes were dull with suffering.

They brought me a mirror and I looked into it. Gazing back at me was a wild, black, high-cheekboned face, like the face of an Indian *fakir*, the hair and beard long and matted. It was perched on a body completely without flesh, the skin stretched black and burned over the ribs, the buttocks completely gone so that all one could see was the framework of the pelvis.

It was for all the world like looking at a charred piece of furniture, some twisted frame salvaged from a fire. But as I laid down the mirror, Doris Lim and I looked at each other and suddenly, for the first time since the torpedo had struck, a smile crossed her face.

We were alive.

8

We spent six weeks on this island of Sipora, only 100 miles from the port of Padang from which we had sailed in the *Rooseboom*. At least half of the six weeks passed before we could feel that we had, even in part, regained our strength.

At first the Malays put us into a hut in which fishing gear, old baskets and dried fish were stored. It was a hut which brought home to us the full significance of that Shakespearean phrase, 'an ancient and a fish-like smell'.

We told the Malays we were husband and wife and must be left together. We suddenly seemed to hate the thought of being parted.

The sores caused by the salt water took a long time to heal, but the island women did their best for us with herbs and ointments.

As the black sunburn began to peel off in patches, leaving us piebald, we presented an odd sight.

Gradually, as her strength came back, Doris Lim became more talkative, and I heard the whole story of the events which had caused her to be a passenger on the *Rooseboom*.

She was born in Shanghai but her parents were dead. As she had been brought up in an American convent, she spoke only a little Chinese.

As far back as 1933, in the early days of Japanese aggression in China, she had been engaged in work for Chinese and British intelligence.

She had been working in Tientsin just prior to the Japanese occupation there, and got out by the skin of her teeth.

Again in Shanghai, she fled just as the Japs came in and made her way to Singapore. There she worked for some time as an assistant to a Chinese news cameraman, the Far East representative of Metro-Goldwyn-Mayer.

As the Japanese siege of Singapore grew more intense, the film man tried to obtain a passage for her to Batavia.

But difficulties of nationality held her up, and she became the responsibility of the British Press Relations Office.

When Singapore fell, five newspapermen who were escaping in the steamer *Kung Wo* took her with them.

The *Kung Wo*, Doris told me, set off from Singapore on Friday, 13 February.

'That was surely asking too much of fate,' she said. 'We were immediately bombed by a Jap plane and lay helpless, just like so many other ships around us, in the midst of the islands.'

They had no lifebelts and no raft, but the whole ship's company, over a hundred of them, made shuttle trips in their one lifeboat to one of the islands.

A destroyer took them to Java. Her companions elected to go

on to Australia but Doris—she never told me why—preferred to join a ship bound for India.

Thus it was that she joined the *Rooseboom* in Batavia, and was aboard her when the ship called at Padang to pick up the rest of us.

Among those people who got in touch with me after my story first appeared in the newspapers was Athole Stewart, an Australian war correspondent who was one of Doris' five companions on the *Kung Wo*.

'What a charming little girl she was,' he said. 'We used to remark how pretty she was, even by European standards.

'When we said goodbye to her in Batavia, we all thought that she was off to safety, and that Australia was going to be the dangerous place.

'Doris had seemed like our mascot during the bad days in Singapore and while we were escaping. She was the kind of girl who makes you marvel at the courage of women.'

One day I put it to Doris that, rather than wait for the Japs to come to the island and find us (as we both knew they would one day), it would be better to push off into the jungle and try to establish ourselves with some natives bent on keeping out of Japanese reach.

She shrugged her shoulders and said, 'What good would it do? How would we live? The natives are all anti-white. None of them can be trusted.'

What will you do, I would ask, when the Japs come?

'I?' she answered. 'I will be killed. You will be all right. You will be a prisoner of war.'

Two races form the population of Sipora: the native Mentawais and the transported Malays.

Most of the land had been parcelled out by the Dutch to the Mentawais, for the Malays were too lazy to be good husbandmen.

The Mentawais did all the cultivation, raising rice, tapioca, peanuts and fruit. They did considerable trade with the Malays on a barter system, bringing along their crops and exchanging them for other necessities.

The average Malay contented himself with a little fishing, and as soon as I felt fit enough, I went on one or two of those fishing trips.

The Malay method was to go out in a small boat, drop one end of a net, then sail round and drop the other end some distance away.

All the inhabitants of the village would then join in pulling the net to the shore, where the catch was shared by everyone.

Later on I took part in many fishing trips with the Mentawais on another part of the island. They were colourful affairs.

The natives paraded through the village late at night with blazing torches, then sailed out into the bay in their *sampans*, torches still ablaze. The light attracted the fish to the surface where they were adroitly speared.

The Mentawais were wonderful marksmen with bow and arrow. Their bows were massive weapons, six feet in length and so powerful that, experimenting with them, I could hardly draw them back. With them the natives would hunt monkey, iguana and small bears in the jungle.

The arrows were tipped with a swift-acting poison prepared by the womenfolk. After an animal had been killed, the flesh had to be cut out where the arrow had impaled it.

One day I saw a Mentawai pick off a monkey at what seemed extraordinary range. So I paced it. It was 112 yards!

The native cooking was done in hollow bamboo shoots. The Mentawais packed the bamboo containers with food, sealed them and threw them on the fire.

Then the bamboo was pulled out, the outer covering stripped off by a smart blow with a machete to reveal the food, ready for eating.

Many of the Mentawais were Christians. They were easy to recognise because they cut their hair in European fashion. They also wore trousers and vests instead of the loincloths and nose ornaments the non-Christians wore.

Doris and I spent the latter part of our stay on Sipora in the chief Mentawai village. This was graced by a pier built by the Dutch and by a main street, Juliana Street, which led from the pier to a medical post the Germans had built before the war.

Right up to the end, I remained an object of tremendous curiosity. My meals were always a public occasion.

Groups of boys and girls came down to watch me eat, amidst much talking, chuckling and sly commentary.

In the end I began to take my audience as much for granted as if they had been an orchestra playing for me in some restaurant!

The Mentawais lived in communities, in huge huts built off the ground on piles twelve feet high.

Some of the huts were over a hundred feet long, housing a number of families in separate cubicles. In a space in the centre of the hut, the council of elders would meet to discuss the affairs of the community.

I was told Mentawai boys and girls usually marry when they are about eleven or twelve. There is a custom of trial marriage whereby, after informing the elders of their intention, a young couple live together experimentally for a fortnight.

If at the end of that time they still want to marry, they do so. If not, the whole affair is off.

Every Mentawai smokes from the very earliest age. One evening I sat in the midst of a chat with two elders of the tribe. I was fascinated when a tiny naked child, who could not have been more than two or three years old, came toddling across to us smoking a huge cigarette rolled from a palm leaf.

One of the elders was sucking an unlit pipe, and the child solemnly approached and offered him a light.

Another peculiarity I found it hard to get used to was the deep tones of the womenfolk and the high-pitched falsetto voices of the men. It was odd to hear a deep guffaw from a woman and then a high-pitched, adolescent-like titter from a man.

I became particularly friendly with the schoolteacher and medical orderly who ran the hospital post.

They were both Bataks and, like all members of that Sumatran race, were gentle-natured and tremendously intelligent.

They treated Doris for malaria, which she had now developed, and they treated the wound in my leg where a piece of metal had remained lodged from the time of the torpedoing until they probed it out.

The broken shoulder had hardly bothered me at all since Mrs Nunn had made her makeshift sling. Even during the clash with the murder gang I had hardly been conscious of it.

Both the *guru* (schoolteacher) and the *mantray* (orderly) were Christians and both, to my delight, knew a fair smattering of English.

Their post was furnished with a church, a medical hut and a stone building used as a hospital.

Daily treatment at the hospital and the generous meals of rice, fish, fried bananas and potatoes which we were given soon began to show results in our general fitness.

But one day I had a shock. A Mentawai—one of the few who ever evinced any hostility towards us—stepped in front of me on a footpath and exclaimed, '*Balanda, sudamati.*' ('White man, you will die.')

They always addressed me by the term they use for the Dutch. '*Balanda*' literally meant 'Redneck', much like the word 'Rooineck' used in South Africa. No matter how many times I explained, 'I am not a Dutchman,' the description persisted.

The Mentawai pointed towards my body and said, '*Beriberi,*' then repeated, '*Sudamati.*'

I hardly realised what he meant, but the two Bataks brought it home to me.

We had been accustomed to receiving huge helpings of rice at their house but now, suddenly, they announced that they had stopped eating rice. We sat down instead to fried bananas, tapioca and baked sago.

The procedure continued for several days and I was puzzled, for I could see signs about the house that rice was being eaten when I was not there.

Then I realised that I was suffering from beriberi, caused by eating polished rice with consequent lack of vitamins. What I had begun to imagine was a pleasing stoutness about my body was the dropsical symptom associated with the disease.

The Bataks, noticing the symptoms and knowing that

continued rice-eating would be fatal to me, had removed rice from their own menu as well as mine rather than tell me that I was ill.

A lassitude began to creep over me about this time, another symptom of the beriberi. I became affected by little things. For example, one day when making my listless way along the beach, I kicked against a thread bobbin and saw the words 'Anchor Mills, Paisley' inscribed upon it.

I rushed to the village headman and told him excitedly that this was from my country, from Scotland.

'No, no—London,' he replied.

Then he told me that the thread was used for repairing their nets. The Dutch imported it to Sumatra, and the natives bought it when they traded on the mainland.

It was a good thread, he told me. The Japanese thread was 'not good thread'.

(Nowadays I live only ten minutes' walk from the Anchor Mills. I contacted them soon after my return to Scotland. I told them of this incident of the bobbin, and was shown around the mills.)

I decided that if I was to die of beriberi it would be as well to leave some record of what had happened to the company of the *Rooseboom*.

So I composed a letter and left it with the Batak, addressed to the commander of whatever British force might some day come to the island.

I told the story of the lifeboat, giving all the names with which I was familiar and recounting the incidents in brief.

I enclosed the names and addresses of relatives, and wrote: *Please notify them and please notify my regiment.*

A few days later, the Japs arrived on Sipora.

Later, years later, I could afford to laugh at the comic figures that the Japanese must have cut to any disinterested spectator as they staged their arrival.

They went through all the motions of an invasion exercise as they landed in the face of nothing more intimidating than a bunch of terrified villagers, whose armoury contained only bows and arrows.

The Japs were patrolling the islands. They arrived in one of the Dutch military steam launches to which they had fallen heir.

As they disembarked, they mounted machine guns on the little pier and trained them on deserted Juliana Street.

Most of the villagers had fled into the jungle but the Japs were determined to impress with a show of might, and a motorcycle patrol raced noisily down the roadway. Behind came two or three dozen soldiers mounted on bicycles, all heavily armed.

The first question the Japanese sergeant in charge of the patrol put to the headman was, 'Where are the white man and his Chinese girl?'

It appeared that the story of our arrival was already fully known at the Japanese headquarters in Padang. They suspected that we had been placed there deliberately to stir up anti-Japanese feeling.

We were marched down the street to the launch where a Japanese officer in a green uniform, top boots and a sword sat at a table on the deck.

The headman explained through an interpreter how we had arrived. He assured the Japs that he had given us just enough sustenance to keep us alive until the patrol appeared.

I heard the interpreter say to the headman in Malay, 'There are other islands to be visited. The prisoners cannot travel in the launch. You will take them to the mainland when the prau which carries the mail makes its next trip. You will be held responsible for their safe delivery.'

Then we had a glimpse of the machine that was the Japanese Occupation in action.

The attendant elders were handed parcels of supplies. They consisted of one tin of condensed milk for each member of the island's population, three or four Japanese flags for each hut and a massive assortment of propaganda leaflets.

The Japanese officer barked a few farewell sentences, which the interpreter translated as a summary of the many kindnesses which the islanders had had at Japanese hands.

It concluded with a further reassurance: that any who did not co-operate would have their heads cut off.

Then the motorcycle patrol came racing up the road, their foolish exhausts making a noise like a speedway meeting. The launch put out to sea again, and the main body of villagers emerged from their hiding places in the jungle.

When we boarded the prau for Padang, there were many tearful farewells from the islanders. There were also a few gestures from some whose sense of humour caused them to point towards the mainland and then significantly draw their fingers across their throats.

On 18 May, just seventy-nine days after we had left Padang in the *Rooseboom*, we arrived back there. As we approached the harbour, I saw with astonishment two white men in white shirts and drill shorts, walking briskly along the seafront.

I had not set eyes on a white face since the Javanese butchered the big gunner, and I cried out and hailed them excitedly.

They were Germans who were, of course, allowed the run of the island.

For four days the Japanese subjected me to a prolonged interrogation. They soon made it evident that the person about whom they most wanted to know was Doris Lim.

Again and again the same questions were fired at me. First in an interview with an English-speaking Malay, then with a stout elderly Jap in a shirt with a *sarong*, then with a tall Japanese with a blood-stained bandage about his head and finally with a shaven-headed officer of the Japanese secret police.

How long had I known Doris Lim?

What was she doing on the *Rooseboom*?

What did I know about her job?

What had she told me on the island?

Was it not strange that she should be the only Chinese national allowed aboard a ship evacuating British soldiers from Malaya?

Finally, fantastically, were we lovers?

All these recurring questions were interspersed with others, from which they sought to identify villages which had helped the fleeing Argylls in Malaya.

Doris Lim, said the police interrogator, had confessed that she had been working against Nippon. I might as well 'come clean' and admit that we were working together, that the British had placed us on the island to foment trouble.

To all these questions I answered, as well I might, in all truth: that I knew nothing about Doris beyond the barest details of towns in which she had lived.

I had never seen or heard of her in my life before she appeared on the *Rooseboom*. I had no idea why she should be aboard.

The Japanese varied their 'softening-up' methods in their usual way.

I was left without food for the last three days of the

interrogation. I spent most of my time in a cell where there was only a floor to lie on, and where a shadeless electric light glared down throughout the night.

There was periodic punching and pummelling by the soldiers who escorted me to the interrogation rooms. The officer with the bandaged head twice flung his chair in my face.

But the most painful of all the 'exercises in tongue-loosening' was when they perched me, kneeling, on a block of wood about three feet long, four feet wide and two feet thick.

I knelt there for what seemed like hours, my hands behind my back and the pain of my uncomfortable position growing more and more excruciating. Each time I moved in an attempt to ease my muscles, one of the guards would strike me in the face. Each time I keeled over, dizzy with pain and exhaustion, I was brought round and the question was repeated: 'What do you know of Doris Lim?'

Eventually it must have dawned on the Japs that I really did not know more than I had said. I was passed on to the prisoner-of-war authorities who were to be my hosts for the three years that followed.

In all this time in Padang I was close to Doris Lim only once. At the end of the first day's interrogation, we were brought together in a kitchen and given a meal of rice and vegetables.

A Japanese soldier tossed us a packet of cigarettes and, quite expressionless and without interrupting his conversation with his companion, leaned across and lit them for us.

Immediately after we had finished our smokes, we were marched to separate cells. I never saw Doris again.

About a week later, as I lay in hospital, one of the medical officers said to me, 'I have a message for you. Someone called Doris Lim. She said to tell you that she is in hospital, still in Padang. She hopes you are well.'

But a month later, after I had been passed as fit and was awaiting transfer to a prison camp, another officer came to me and said, 'I'm afraid there's bad news about that Chinese girl you talk about, Gibson. They tell me she's been shot.'

And every inquiry I have made since then—in Singapore at the end of the war, among various authorities since I came home and among the people who knew her before she joined the *Rooseboom*—has elicited no further clue to her fate than that.

9

After three years of observing that strangest of human characters, the Japanese, I was no nearer to understanding him than I had been at the first encounter. Perhaps it was because, being his prisoner, I could not form an objective viewpoint.

No standards of Western logic could be applied to his conduct. One moment, after giving you cause to reflect that he was perhaps, after all, just an ordinary not-quite-so-bad-as-painted human being, he would become a raging, demoniac ape.

From my cell in the interrogation offices I was taken to the prisoner-of-war encampment in Padang. I arrived there barefoot, holding up my native trousers with one hand.

A month later the whole camp, consisting of some 1,600 British, Dutch and Eurasians, was shifted by lorry to Medan, North Sumatra. It was a 900-mile journey which took five days.

On the way we came to a point on the road which had special significance. It was indicated by marks on the cliffs which rose on either side of us.

It was the Equator.

The Japanese guards immediately ordered us to descend from the lorries, walk across the Equator and then embus again.

One of the lorries skidded over at a precipitous part of the road, and all the prisoners in it were injured.

In hospital they were visited by a Japanese general, complete with retinue and two A.D.C.s carrying fruit and flowers!

The general solemnly addressed the injured, offering apologies in the name of the Imperial and Invincible Nipponese Army, and assuring them that the driver would be severely punished for the carelessness that had endangered their lives.

Prisoners from the Argylls were, at this time, located in two main groups: those captured before the fall of Singapore who were held at Kuala Lumpur, and those taken at Singapore who were kept on the island at Changi.

But there were also hundreds of us in Sumatra or Java who had escaped to these islands or been captured at sea.

The Japs' lack of shipping prevented us from being moved, as they would have wished, to work on the infamous Bangkok–Moulmein railway in Thailand.

I was in the Medan camp for two years.

For the first six months the camp was under the command of an odd character, a major past middle age who spent most of his time in a drunken haze.

Each morning at seven he would take roll call, wearing pyjamas, a military cap and his sword.

He was, like so many of the Japanese, a homosexual, and a

number of prisoners were beaten up for resisting his advances.

On his more maudlin days he would tell us, sadly and to all intents and purposes benevolently, how unhappy our misdemeanours had made him.

Then he would make a prisoner stand to attention in front of him while he swung his big two-handed sword above his victim's head, stopping the blade within what literally was a hair's-breadth.

To all who flinched—and I saw only one who did not—the major delivered a lecture on timidity.

The one who stood perfectly still while the sword whirled above him was a Dutchman. Our bibulous major shook him by the hand, slapped him on the back and presented him with a prize of fruit and cigarettes.

From the beginning the major insisted that the roll call numbering-off be in Japanese. One would hear '*itchi, ni, san*' ('one, two, three') followed by the English 'four' from some forgetful or defiant individual.

Then the corporal would curse us as 'bugaros' (fools), slap number four in the face and make us start again. If he was lucky he got us up to seven, and then went through the same performance again.

On the whole, things were bearable under the rule of our first commandant, but he was replaced and Koreans were substituted for Japs as guards.

The Koreans, themselves terrified of the Japanese, excelled their masters in inflicting brutality on the prisoners. Those of us who refused to sign non-escape forms were forced into submission by starvation and thirst—we were left for five days without food or water.

On our first Christmas, however, we were each issued with ten cigarettes, a glass of wine and extra rations.

And that is the odd thing. Now that the years have passed, one remembers the pleasant moments, the amusing moments. I think because they were outstanding in the grimness of our existence.

Nowadays I sometimes meet up with men I knew in Medan, and always our talk turns to the things about the Japs which made us laugh.

One prisoner whom we recall is Captain Pat Kirkwood of the I.M.S., a Highlander from Forres whose tall and black-bearded figure came to be regarded by the Nips with positive awe.

He treated them with complete disdain. Even when the senior British officer mistakenly, we felt, ordered him to shave off his beard, the Japs' respect was only slightly lessened.

Kirkwood was six feet and three inches tall. Even the Japs seemed to find it funny when he and I, who had become very friendly, used to pace around the wire together, he exactly ten and a half inches taller than I was.

Let me describe an incident which was typical of Kirkwood.

Once, he was shaving outside the hut when a small and self-important Japanese guard approached. Rules said that we always had to bow to our guards but Kirkwood, with the merest glance, continued shaving.

The Jap cursed angrily but Kirkwood just looked at him contemptuously, indicated that he was shaving and testily waved the Nip out of existence.

Positively screaming with rage, the guard brought his rifle and bayonet to an on-guard position and lunged at Kirkwood's stomach.

In a flash the doctor's long left arm shot out. His great sinewy hand grasped the collar of the Nip's tunic and the guard was swung clean off his feet.

Kirkwood calmly relieved him of his rifle and bayonet, which he propped against the hut. Holding the small Jap out at arm's length, he proceeded to deliver a lecture in broadest Scots, culminating in a declaration that if the Jap annoyed him again, he would skelp his bum very hard indeed.

The Jap, almost black in the face and frothing with rage, was then lowered to the ground and told to run along and behave himself.

The story swept round the camp like wildfire, and there was considerable perturbation as the sentry was observed to be making his way to the guardroom.

Sure enough, out came a squad of six, headed by an N.C.O.

with drawn sword who came marching towards our hut.

The little sentry pointed to Kirkwood who was marched off under escort to the guardroom.

The rest of us spent a very unhappy hour, for we knew how summarily others had been decapitated for annoying the Japs.

Then towards us came strolling the familiar figure of Kirkwood, alive and whole in his white shirt with Red Cross armband and his Boy-Scout-type shorts.

'What happened?' we demanded. 'Are you all right? What did they do to you?'

'Of course I'm all right,' said Kirkwood. 'They didn't do anything. They've just told me that it is a very serious offence to disarm a sentry. In fact, it appears that it is punishable by death. They have asked me not to do it again.'

Several times we saw the Japs predilection for making the punishment fit the crime.

They were tremendously scared of fire, and smoking was sternly restricted to certain times and certain places. When we smoked we had to carry an ashtray.

One of the prisoners, a middle-aged Dutchman, was caught smoking out of regulation hours. Straightaway he was placed in front of the guardroom, pipe in mouth and a pile of black, strong tobacco at his feet. He was ordered to start smoking and not to stop.

As soon as he finished one pipe he was ordered to fill another. The process went on for hours, while the sun climbed high and a guard of six stood impassively watching him.

The Dutchman turned a dirty green, was violently sick and passed out several times, only to be roused and ordered to continue smoking.

At last, completely exhausted by his retching, he lay, unable to hold the pipe any more in his mouth. The corporal administered a final slap and a warning not to smoke out of hours again.

Then there was an occasion when a soldier was caught eating fruit in the garden which we cultivated and which the Japs harvested.

He was ordered to pick about a dozen papayas (fruit about the size of melons). We were paraded and given an example of what would happen to anyone who ate Nipponese-owned fruit.

'Start eating,' he was told.

After he had finished four of the papayas, he indicated with a wan smile that he could eat no more. He was immediately clouted with a rifle butt and ordered, 'Eat on.'

More and more of the fruit was stuffed into him till we thought he would burst. First he was sick, then he indicated to the guards that he desired to evacuate.

He was told to do so on the spot, and then eat on.

Finally, as he lay half-unconscious and deathly pale, the Japs delivered their usual lecture to us and ordered him back to quarters.

One of the most extraordinary incidents occurred when the Medan camp began to run short of food. The Japs issued rifles and five rounds of ammunition each to some fifty prisoners, and ordered them to go out and hunt for wild pig!

At Christmas time they would become drunk and friendly.

One Christmas morning, a Dutch doctor asked me to help him collect some parcels of food which he had arranged to have smuggled into the camp from a Chinese outside (a Chinese who later, we learned, was executed for his anti-Japanese activities).

The parcels were to be thrown over the wall at a certain time when there were usually no Nips near that part of the camp.

Unfortunately, on this morning of all mornings, a sentry elected to start pacing the chosen stretch of wall a few minutes before the appointed time.

The doctor engaged him in conversation while I stood discreetly in the background. The sentry answered sullenly and suspiciously.

I saw the doctor glance at his watch, and knew that any minute now the parcels were due to arrive.

The doctor tried to divert attention by walking slowly away from the wall, still talking to the Jap in Malay.

But it was no use. Bang on time, flung with all the aim and precision of an expert grenade thrower, a parcel came sailing over the wall and landed almost at the feet of the sentry.

Then another and another and another. Time, as far as the doctor and I were concerned, seemed to stand still.

From over the wall came a voice which said, '*Salaamat muchan, tuan.*' ('Good eating, master.')

Then silence. We gazed at the sentry and the sentry gazed at us. Our trepidation, I am certain, was only equalled by his astonishment.

'*Ini apah?*' he exclaimed at last in a tone which I took to give his words the meaning, 'What the bloody hell is all this?'

'*Sedikit sedikit muchan, ini hari Kerismas,*' answered the doctor. ('Just a little food as this is Christmas Day.')

The Nip gazed at us blankly for a moment. Then, slowly, he drew in his breath and just as slowly nodded. '*Ah soka! Kerismas.*'

He waved his hand. '*Sahaya tao.*' ('I understand.')

He grinned and indicated that we should pick up the parcels. '*Sayah tedah mata,*' he said. ('I don't see anything.')

We profoundly uttered, '*Arigato*' ('Thank you') many times and accompanied our thanks with ceremonial bows. It seemed no time for dignity—or even for racial feeling!

For the rest, those days in Medan seem very far away now. There was monotony, feuds, jealousy and antipathy between British and Dutch, British and Australians, and Australians and Dutch. There were beatings and beheadings. There was news from Europe on our secret radios. In the end, the Japs quite openly discussed the war situation with us because they knew we were more familiar with what was happening than they were.

In June 1944 I, along with 743 other P.O.W.s, embarked on the cargo steamer *Van Wyck*, thirty-three years old and swarming with rats. What our destination was to be we did not know. We presumed Thailand.

But whatever it was to be did not matter, because forty-eight hours out from Sumatra I found myself, for the second time, treading water while a torpedoed ship went down!

We had been in a convoy of eight, the others mainly tankers carrying high-octane spirit to Singapore. We had had an escort of three bombers and four river gunboats.

The Allied submarine commander, whoever he was, got five of the convoy. Glory be!

When our ship was struck by two torpedoes, it literally fell to pieces. Seventeen Japanese and 113 prisoners were killed or drowned.

Twelve Dutchmen pulled off a feat which makes the performances of the Channel swimmers who spend weeks in training seem pretty poor stuff. Gaunt and only half fit after their years of captivity, they actually swam twelve miles to the Sumatran mainland, making a concerted and deliberate attempt to reach freedom.

The fact that a Jap patrol, warned by airspotters who had

observed them, was waiting for them on the shore, made their attempt none the less gallant.

The only tanker left from the convoy picked up survivors and took us, after a couple of days of grilling on its iron deck, to Singapore.

And in Singapore it was, in August 1945, that the forces of freedom, storming back after three and a half years of absence, discovered us and brought us home.

10

Some of my fellow Argylls have suggested that I should include a last chapter in this chronicle: the story of the six-week jungle march by which I and two others escaped to Sumatra after the disastrous Battle of Slim River. It was a battle which proved to be the breaking point for the Argylls in the Malayan campaign of January 1942.

In the history of the 2nd Battalion of the Argylls and of the part they played in Malaya, you can read that parties of soldiers who had been cut off struggled on after the Slim battle, enmeshed in the jungle, starving, fever-stricken and exhausted but refusing to surrender.

You can read that some of the Argylls, 'among them Captain Bardwell, Lieutenant Montgomery Campbell, Platoon-Sergeant-Major Colvin, Captain Broadhurst, Sergeant Gibson, Lance-Corporal Gray and Corporal Robertson, made their way to the coast, got fishing boats and sailed to Sumatra'.

I am that Sergeant Gibson.

Captain Broadhurst and Lance-Corporal Gray were the two men who emerged from the jungle with me a month after Slim.

We were the only three to get through out of an original

column of nearly 300 men.

Remember, if you can, what was happening in those far-off days.

Our battalion of the Argylls was part of the 12th Indian Infantry Brigade under Brigadier Paris. From 14 December 1941 until 7 January 1942, the date of the Battle of Slim River, we had faced the enemy continuously in a retreating fight which has become a legend of the Far East.

When our fighting began, the Japs were coming hell for leather through the peninsula; the 11th Indian Division had been defeated at Jitra; with the sinking of the *Prince of Wales* and *Repulse*, Britain had lost command of the sea; our air force had been almost completely destroyed.

At one time or another during the three-week campaign, there was a total of 940 men of all ranks in the battalion. Of those 940 men, 244 were lost, killed or missing in action; more than 150 were wounded; and 184 men died as prisoners of war.

Other pens better suited than mine have told the whole brave story of that retreat down the peninsula to Singapore. But no one yet has told the strange story of the bid for freedom that was made by the shattered remnants of 'B' and 'C' companies, 2nd Argylls.

We remnants set out on the morning of 7 January, the morning that followed the Jap breakthrough at Slim.

Captain Ian Lapsley had formed and taken command of the escaping column.

He was an ex-cricket captain of Hillhead High School, Glasgow; a handsome, quick-thinking, popular young officer. Supporting him were Captain Tim Turner, Captain D. Drummond-Hay (shot in the knee), Lieutenant K. I. McLeod and Second-Lieutenant J. J. Colliston. Their first roll call made the total strength of the column to be just under 300 men.

For two days we hacked our way south, aiming to get to Tanjong Malim which we had calculated would be the next position of the battalion. We could not know that the Japanese were already there!

Our wounded—Drummond-Hay, Private McKnight with a bayonet wound in his back, Private Stewart, shot through both wrists—were magnificent. How Drummond-Hay, with a bullet in his knee, climbed and scrambled over rocks, hillsides and undergrowth disdaining a stretcher, I cannot tell.

Early on the morning of the 9th we were joined by Captain D. K. Broadhurst, an officer of the Straits Settlements Police. He had already been attached to the Argylls a month back at Baling.

When the Japs broke through and passed him at Slim, he was with the 5th/2nd Punjabis, and escaped into the jungle with some Indians.

He spent the night soaking wet, resting in open rubber; ran for it after coming face to face with a group of Japs on bicycles;

and marched throughout the next day with an English gunner and a solitary Argyll, Private Johnson, with whom he had caught up.

Now here he was, thin, sallow, dirty, unshaven and tired but with a cheerful, casual undisturbed phlegm which we were to witness many times before the march was over.

Broadhurst was a cool customer. As we ran through a banana plantation to escape a pursuing Jap patrol, I saw him pause to pluck some of the fruit while Lapsley called on him, for God's sake, to get a move on.

He was a fluent speaker of the Malayan tongue, Cantonese and other Chinese dialects. His presence was to stand us in good stead.

Quite suddenly during the third day, Drummond-Hay announced that we must leave him.

Neither he nor anyone else had put it into words that he was holding up the column, but everyone knew that it was so. His gesture was accepted in the spirit in which he made it.

One of the soldiers declared that he, too, could go no further and would like to stay with Drummond-Hay.

So we handed them over to the care of a Tamil estate manager who promised to hide and feed them until they were fit again.

Captain Drummond-Hay was captured, survived the prison camp and the Thai Railway, and was among those Argylls who reached home again.

Most of the columns were now desperate with hunger, for all we had to subsist on were raw bananas and such sugar cane as was available.

Once, some of us came on a group of Indian soldiers cooking chicken and rice, of which they gave us some mouthfuls.

Mostly, though, we were fortified by the thought that the rest of the battalion would be waiting for us at Tanjong Malim. We were sure they would have the pot a-boiling.

At nightfall on 11 January we had a stroke of luck. We met some Chinese at a charcoal burner's hut, and they conducted us down to their village and sold us a pig. I remember the price was $18!

Private Harvey, a regimental cook, and Campbell, a stretcher bearer, assisted with the slaughter. They used bayonets and parangs and the noise might have been heard in Singapore.

Broadhurst sat up most of the night cutting the pig into sections, and it was cooked laboriously over a charcoal stove. The liver and other choice portions were given to the wounded and the worst-off amongst our sick.

Then the portions were handed over to the warrant officers and sergeants to distribute as fairly as possible.

It rained heavily that night, and dozens tried to squeeze into the charcoal hut for shelter.

Next morning at dawn we set off again, all belching greasy pig and all vastly improved in spirit.

Our hopes were short-lived. Later that day we sighted Tanjong Malim from the top of a hill, only to learn from Chinese and Malays who met us as we advanced that the British troops had passed through forty-eight hours before. The Japanese were now in occupation.

The Malays guided us down to the bank of the Bernam River where, bearded and filthy, Lapsley and others among us seized their first chance in days to bathe and shave.

There are spells in the march immediately after this which are vague to me, for about this time I suffered such a severe attack of malaria that I felt I had to throw in my hand. Lapsley coaxed me to carry on.

I remember collapsing in a shivering, sobbing heap, saying hysterically to Lapsley to leave me my compass and revolver. I would catch up with him when I was better.

Lapsley coaxed, cursed, cajoled and comforted me until, God knows how, I was on my feet, clinging to him and staggering on.

Since my return to Britain I have been able to see extracts from Broadhurst's diary. They reveal that our progress during those succeeding days was, briefly:

'*Afternoon of 12 January. Pushed along a track which Malays said would take us to Kuala Kubu. Got hopelessly mixed as the track disappeared. Spent hours cutting through dense jungle and finishing up where we started from. Found a likely track and spent the night on the bank of Bernam River.'*

'Morning of 13 January. Continued along the newly discovered track. Climbed 2,000 feet, found the going too hard, made for ground level again and came near the road at Kalumpang. Here watched the heavy Jap transports on their way along the road. Marched on to Kerling and spent the night in a Chinese hut.'

'Fourteenth January. Reached Kuala Kubu where we lost Ian Lapsley.'

From the beginning Lapsley kept me at his side at the head of the column. One of my chief qualifications was that I was an especially good map reader due to my long spells with Battalion and Brigade Intelligence.

As we approached a village, therefore, it became procedure for the column to halt some distance away. Broadhurst (with his lingual powers), Lapsley and me went ahead to see what we could procure in the way of food.

Most of the time we were all in a half-starved state, chewing at whatever we could lay our hands on.

There was tapioca but it was very different from the puddings that mother made! We had to pull up the long thick roots with their purplish poisonous skins, skin and boil them, and eat the result which tasted like potato.

We also ate unripe bananas. They, too, were boiled in their skins and tasted much like potato.

Bamboo shoots tossed into a pot with a handful of slugs made us a 'jungle stew'.

Every now and again a party would break off and go foraging. Several did not rejoin us again.

I recall once there was nearly a riot at a Malay *kampong*. Some of our lads found a hidden store of rice, an 'iron ration', and set about looting it.

The Malays prepared to defend their food and it needed all the tact of Lapsley with the troops, and the diplomacy of Broadhurst with the villagers, to avert fresh trouble.

Another time we met a Chinese who promised, on payment of $50, to guide us to Kuala Lumpur along a jungle track which would take fifty miles off our journey.

Everyone was jubilant. We thought we would stand a good chance of getting to our own lines at last. We scraped together the money and handed it over. We would set off first thing in the morning.

Just before we turned in, I chatted with Captain Lapsley. He told me that when we reached Singapore, he was to be married. I would be invited; there would be 'lashings to eat and drink ...'

He woke me before dawn and sent me to rouse the troops and guide.

But the guide could not be found. I searched for nearly an hour before I returned to Lapsley.

He was speechless with rage. Not only had the guide gone

but so had five members of the column. (Four, I may say, were now dead.)

'If I lay my hands on them,' raged Lapsley, 'I'll shoot the lot.'

Word of the latest blow spread round. Some received it with anger, others greeted it apathetically.

On we went ...

Ian Lapsley, our most inspirational member, parted from us strangely.

We had reached Kuala Lumpur after a week's marching. He and I had crept forwards in the usual way to spy out the land as we approached the village.

The column was lying in the cover of a rubber plantation.

We scrutinised the district officer's bungalow with our binoculars, and then went forward cautiously. The house was empty but there was evidence that Japs had been there.

Most important, from our point of view, was a store of rations which the Japanese had ignored. A large quantity of bully beef, jam, biscuits and the like.

We swallowed a few swift mouthfuls. Then Lapsley told me to return to the column with as much as I could carry. I was to tell Captain Turner to bring the column down to the road, ready to cross. I then had to return for Lapsley and the remainder of the rations.

I followed his instructions but when I got back to the bungalow there was no sign of Lapsley. I went through the house from top to bottom, shouting his name. He had vanished and there was no single trace of where he had gone.

I took it that he must have gone back on his own to rejoin the column, and that we had missed each other in passing.

Meanwhile the company moved for half an hour, then halted. After they had waited some time for us to return, Captain Turner and Broadhurst came back in search of us.

I was lost but they traced me by my shouts.

Everyone, of course, was greatly perturbed by Lapsley's disappearance. We hung on for a considerable time, hoping that he would turn up. Then Turner began to worry about staying too long in one place for Jap patrols were always on the go, and it was decided that we had to march on.

I was not to see Ian Lapsley alive again. But we were to learn what happened to him.

Several days further on in our journey, at a place called Gombak, near Kuala Lumpur, we fell in with a bearded ragged Argyll named Fitzpatrick. At Kuala Kubu, he had been with a rear section of the column.

Lapsley, said Fitzpatrick, joined this other section just after losing us. 'And he wanted to know why the hell you hadn't waited for him.'

Lapsley, it transpired, had sat finishing his meal after I left him at the bungalow. He was eating from a tin of bully beef when he heard footsteps which he presumed were mine.

He looked up, his mouth still full, and found himself gazing at four Japanese officers, whose faces registered an astonishment at least equal to his.

Ian was the first to recover and the first to act.

He hurled his bully-beef tin into their faces, dived from the room and raced into the jungle as their pistols cracked behind him.

After lying low and then seeking in vain for the column, he first fell in with some gunners. Next, he joined Fitzpatrick's section and then, in company with several other Argylls, he fell in with one of the Chinese guerrilla bands.

It was fighting alongside those guerrillas that Ian Lapsley, like so many of his fellows, died of attrition and jungle disease. He was a very brave officer and a lovable comrade.

We were in a pitiful state as we approached Kuala Lumpur. Dysentery, tropical ulcers, fever, starvation, exposure, exhaustion and concomitant mental ills had all taken their toll.

The column must have lost two thirds of its original strength, for there seemed no alternative to the rule of 'march or die'. Colliston had gone, so had McLeod. Captain Tim Turner was the only officer left.

He, Broadhurst, the remaining warrant officers and all we

surviving N.C.O.s held a conference to decide what had to be done.

At the conference there were some who said stick together and others who declared that we should split up into small parties.

Those in favour of splitting up argued the difficulties of feeding a large number, and the difficulties of getting around Kuala Lumpur, now occupied by the Japs.

The situation was put to the troops and, after much argument, it was decided to split into parties of twelve and go off at intervals.

We had three compasses. One was given to Sergeant McKinnon, another to P.S.M. Sloane and the third was retained by me.

Harsh things have been said since about the split-up, and it has been argued that had the column stayed intact more might have got through.

But at that time I was convinced, like so many others, that to break up was the only course which offered even the possibility of getting through. I was one of its advocates then and in no way do I now wish to dissociate myself from it.

At the beginning there were only six in our party after the split-up. However, we were joined that evening by six more: Lieutenant Ronnie Marriott of the Argylls, Major O'Neill of the I.M.S., two divisional signallers (one of them, I recall, named Sigley) and two gunners, named Lewis and Williams.

Others in our party of twelve included Turner, Broadhurst,

C.S.M. Porter and C.Q.M.S. 'Hookie' Walker.

Major O'Neill's feet were in bad shape. He had no boots and was tramping along with his feet wrapped in sacking. But he remained the irrepressible Irishman, declaring that all we were short of was a damned good feed and a bottle of John Jamieson.

'Then we'll soon be out of this mess,' he said.

But on 17 January, when we were in the region of the Batu Caves, near Kuala Lumpur, our little party was further crippled by an encounter with a Jap patrol to whom Tamil coolies had betrayed us.

We had just finished cutting our way through a particularly nasty piece of jungle, and had been on the scrounge for food round some Malay houses.

Young Ronnie Marriott found a bicycle lying spare and scared the life out of a bunch of Tamils by dashing in amongst them on it.

The Malays from whom we begged food would hardly talk to us. They knew that if they were caught helping us, they would lose their heads on the spot.

But if, they said, we would hide some way from the house, they would bring us food.

We lay down among some young rubber, screened from the main plantation by a small hedge, and within minutes, exhausted, we had all dozed off.

I was awakened by a noise which sounded as if all the fireworks in China were being let off by my ear.

Japs!

We hared blindly through the rubber, with bullets whistling about us, crossed a stream and raced up the side of a hill.

I flung myself into the thick undergrowth, and crashes around me indicated that others of our party had chosen the same spot.

When we were able to take stock, we found there were only six of us: Broadhurst, Porter, Sigley, Lewis, Williams and myself.

Walker, not as quick off his mark, had been captured. He had been seen standing with his hands up. O'Neill had been seen to stumble and fall, presumably shot. Turner had been seen going like a bat out of hell for the rubber.

We lay doggo until dark, and then made our way again towards the Malay houses.

We walked into two of the Malays, and I was all for cutting their throats. I was sure that it must have been they who had passed on word to the Japs.

Broadhurst, however, joined them in conversation. They declared excitedly that it was the Tamils and not they who were to blame.

All they wanted to do was help, they said. There was a hut in the jungle in which they would hide us.

All these Malay *kampongs* had such secret huts in the jungle.

They were for the purpose of hiding their womenfolk from the Japs.

We were pretty well all in but after the Malays had given us a meal of rice and condensed milk, and a piece of sugar cane to chew, we were able to make our way to the jungle hut.

As we approached it we could see the glow of a fire, and our guides gave a low, warning whistle. They said there were already three more soldiers hiding there.

They turned out to be three Argylls: Lance-Corporal Jock Gray, Lance-Corporal Hugh Falls and Private Johnson. We stayed there for some days, all of us very weak. I suffered another malarial relapse and Sigley was so done that he could hardly stir from the floor.

The Malays brought us food, gave us a New Testament to read and regaled us with stories of atrocity.

Then came a further split-up. Broadhurst, Gray, Johnson and I determined to push on; the others decided that they could go no further.

As we said our goodbyes, Sigley gave me his mother's address, handed me his fountain pen and asked me to see her when I reached home. Falls handed me his wristwatch.

I asked them, 'If you think I can get through with these things, why not come with us?' But they could not be persuaded.

So now we were four and one of us, Johnson, was a very sick man indeed.

We tramped on, begging food, stopping at various huts and hiding at any hint of danger.

Once, we traded all the remnants of our possessions to the Malays for a road map; once, I remember, for a tin of sausages, army rations.

The road map and my compass were invaluable. One day we covered as much as ten miles. On most others it would be no more than two or three miles.

The Chinese were invariably kind. I remember, in particular, the way we were cared for at a Chinese tin mine at which we spent a day.

At this time, remember, the Japanese were shooting and beheading wholesale any Chinese whom they suspected of helping the British in any way.

Later, indeed, we were to learn what had happened to Captain Turner, and how a Chinese police clerk named Siow Ah Kiew was beheaded for aiding him.

Mr J. B. Masefield of the Malayan Police told the story. He was a prisoner in Changi camp when Captain Turner and five other Argylls arrived there. They were all in a dishevelled state with long hair, beards and suffering badly from malaria.

Turner must have joined up with the others after his flight from the patrol. They got as far as Benut, on the west coast of Johore, and for a fortnight Ah Kiew sent them food and quinine.

He provided them, too, with a shotgun and ammunition, and set about trying to get them a boat to carry them to Sumatra.

One night his daughter arrived after dark with a note from Mrs Ah Kiew. Her husband, with twenty other Chinese in Benut, had been taken off by the Japanese and executed.

Soon afterwards, Captain Turner and his men were surrounded in their hut and taken prisoner. Turner died of cholera in Siam in 1943.

For us, the outstanding instances of Chinese aid came in the first days of February, when we had Johnson at the end of his tether.

As we limped slowly through a village, a Malay came running to us and begged us not to carry on in that direction. Anti-British elements in the *kampong* had passed on word to a Jap patrol, which was waiting for us at the roadside.

Broadhurst insisted that we take the warning so I picked out a new route on the map. We made our way through a coconut grove towards a Chinese village which we reached about nine in the evening.

The change of direction had been one of those odd twists of fate which are now so fascinating to look back on.

As we sat in weary silence, we heard a child's voice say excitedly in English, 'Where are they? Where are they?'

A little boy, perhaps six or seven years old, appeared hand in hand with a young Chinese nurse.

'Hello,' he said. 'Are you British soldiers?'

We rose to reply and the small boy cried excitedly, 'It's Mr Broadhurst, oh goody, Mr Broadhurst!'

He was the son of a couple, a doctor and his wife, whom Broadhurst had known well in the state of Kedah before the war.

It transpired that mother and son were staying with a Chinese doctor named Koo, who produced a meal, sweets and a bottle of whisky.

Then Dr Koo looked at Johnson and shook his head gravely. 'That man,' he said, 'is unfit to go any further.'

Quite apart from general exhaustion from which we were all suffering, Johnson had developed pneumonia as well as malaria.

But it was impossible to stay any longer in the house. The Japs, who were demanding the doctor's services, could have arrived at any moment. We had to get back to the jungle.

Johnson insisted on accompanying us and off we set, bearing with us fresh rations, sweets, whisky and medicine.

We had not gone very far before we asked a Chinese for directions. He suggested that we follow him to the home of his brother-in-law. 'He will be glad to help you,' he said.

We followed him to a comfortable-looking Chinese house, where we were greeted by three men. They were brothers named Chow, owners of a big music emporium in Singapore.

They spoke good English, and told us that we had to rest there.

We could not stay in the house because the wife of one of them was expecting a baby. However, they said they would be happy to put a hut at the bottom of the garden for our disposal.

We stayed there for many days. I remember that passage of our flight more clearly, perhaps, than any other.

The Chinese brothers brought blankets for Johnson and sacking for ourselves. They furnished us with candles and a portable gramophone. One of the wives washed our ragged clothing, and we shaved and bathed in a nearby stream.

We lay drying in the sun, smoking our cigarettes. Each of us had a drink from Dr Koo's half-bottle and life seemed better then than it had done for many a day.

But Johnson grew no better. I went to him and said, 'Johnny, you're a very sick man.'

'That's okay, Hoot. I'll make it after a wee rest,' he replied.

I told him frankly that we did not think he could, that his only chance was to pack in now and trust himself to the Jap doctors. Jock Gray had said he would go with him.

'No,' said Johnson. 'If I've come as far as this, I'll stick it now.'

Then, after a long pause, he gave me a look I shall never forget and said, 'Don't leave me, Hoot. Don't leave me.'

'We won't leave you, son,' I said.

So there we stayed, taking it in turns to lie beside him until the end, to give him comfort and warmth.

On the night before he died, I had a sudden realisation of the full drama of our situation.

There we were, the moon shining clear on us as we sat by the hut. Up in the Chinese home, a life was coming into the world; here in the hut, a life was ebbing away. We had the gramophone playing, and one of the records the Chinese had given us had the song 'Ye Banks and Braes O' Bonny Doon'.

Broadhurst, Gray and I (I take the dates from Broadhurst's diary) stayed on at this village of Ulu Lungat until 3 February.

Then we pushed on, travelling mainly at night because the roads were freer then. We made the following stops: 4 February, Kachau; 5 February, a hut in the jungle; 6 and 7 February, Broga: 8 and 9 February, Nangi: 10 February, Batang Benar. Finally on 13 February we emerged on the coast at Chuah, just six miles from Port Dickson from which the Argylls had set off to battle two months before.

Once again Broadhurst was our interpreter and negotiator. It was he who arranged to find us a *sampan* with a sympathetic Chinese at Chuah.

There was one preliminary necessity before we sailed for Sumatra, however, and that was to procure a supply of opium for our Chinese boatman, who was an addict.

We dozed at intervals through the night. When we woke it was to find the Sumatran coast close by, the water lapping round our feet at the bottom of the leaky *sampan*. The boatman was oblivious to all about him, steering a glassy-eyed, automatic course.

On 21 February we reached Padang.

We had come through the march in astonishingly good shape, considering everything. I had a swollen body which later I was to recognise as a symptom of beriberi. But I had escaped the jungle sores, the great open ulcers from which both Gray and Broadhurst were suffering.

Jock Gray, whose calmness was proverbial in the regiment, had taken every ordeal as it came with undisturbed phlegm.

During those latter stages when Broadhurst and I would clash over the choice of road to be followed, we would turn to Jock to demand his opinion. He would grin, shrug his shoulders, point out that each route held equally good and equally bad possibilities and then say, 'Please yourselves, as long as we keep getting on.'

Captain Broadhurst reached Australia safely in one of the evacuee ships. He returned later, was parachuted into the jungle during the later phases of the Far East war and finished up a lieutenant colonel.

Some of the other Argylls who were not members of our column got through the jungle to the coast. I know that Platoon-Sergeant-Major F. Colvin stole a fishing boat and sailed it to Sumatra. He had trained the Pioneer Platoon to be up to rifle-platoon standard in the jungle and was, in addition, an amateur yachtsman.

Captain M. E. Bardwell escaped with him and insisted on being flown back to Singapore from Sumatra. There he married, rejoined the regiment in the battle of Singapore and was taken prisoner.

On arriving in Sumatra, Captain Ernest Gordon decided to turn back and run a ferry service for women and children stranded on the islands. He was later captured 1,000 miles to the west, sailing a fishing boat to Ceylon.

Two other Argylls, Private Stewart and Private Bennett, actually stayed on uncaptured in the jungle for four years. In that time they acted as training instructors to Chinese guerrilla forces.

So few who lived ... so many who died ...

I feel I have told their stories without adornment. I have chronicled the events starkly, for it was starkly that they occurred.

Today, anyone who visits the Church of Scotland building in Singapore will find a memorial tablet, erected there to the 'everlasting fame' of the Argylls who served in Malaya. It is with the lines from this tablet that I will end.

'Still, when a chief dies bravely,
We bind with green one wrist—
Green for the brave, for heroes

One crimson thread we twist.
Say ye, oh gallant Hillman,
For these, whose life has fled,
Which is the fitting colour,
The green one or the red?'

Read more about Doris Lim

Learn more about the fate of Doris Lim through an excerpt from the book
Sold for Silver: An autobiography of a girl sold into slavery in Southeast Asia
by Janet Lim (Monsoon Books, Singapore)

As narrated by Janet Lim, a World War Two P.O.W. in Japanese-occupied Sumatra, Indonesia, who was allowed by the Japanese to run a clinic at Indaroeng Cement Factory in West Sumatra:

Not long after my return [to Indaroeng Cement Factory, in August 1944], a Chinese girl, Doris Lim, who was a survivor of a shipwreck during the evacuation from Singapore, came to help me in the clinic. Together we did what we could for the health of the villagers but so many of their customs were most unhygienic.

In our times off duty we tried to help the community in other ways. I was asked if I could teach the Chinese children their language. I only knew about a hundred Chinese characters and told them that it was therefore impossible for me to become a teacher of Chinese. Before the war I had taught in Sunday School and also had taught the Brownies in Singapore, but I felt that a Chinese class was beyond me. However, the Chinese residents pestered me to try, so I gave way and started with a class of twenty-four pupils ranging from six to fourteen years of age. I was paid with three pounds of rice and one pound of sugar a month. We began with a Japanese song; this was compulsory. Unfortunately my Chinese class lasted for only a few months because, when I had finished teaching them what I knew, I had nothing more to contribute to their knowledge.

At this time I was not at all well. One doctor said that I was suffering from general weakness, another that I had contracted tuberculosis. Both agreed that I needed a complete rest and the Japanese were most generous in allowing me to stop work for two months while continuing to pay me the usual salary. Twice a week I went to Padang for vitamin injections. After two months an X-ray was taken of my lungs and it was found that I was clear of tuberculosis; this greatly relieved my mind. I had put on some weight, so I went back to work and for the next twelve months life moved on in comparative calm.

In 1944 tension increased in Indaroeng. Many more Japanese had come and there was much military activity. A.A. guns had sprung up on all sides and soldiers guarded the factory. The Japanese believed that the Americans would attack the factory and said that it was the only undamaged one in Japanese-occupied territory. Wakamatsu, whom I had not seen for a long time, came to see me, as he was going away soon. When we started talking about the war he looked uneasy.

'Wakamatsu San, do you now admit that you are losing the war?'

'No, you are wrong.'

'We are friends and therefore I dare to speak to you like this. A year ago there were hardly any troops in Indaroeng; now the place is swarming with soldiers. You are expecting bombing, aren't you? Please tell me because I do not want to be killed by the Americans.'

'You must be a spy since you seem to know so much.'

'I wish I were; a spy is always a clever person.' He changed the subject.

'I am leaving tomorrow and I hope to be able to send you a postcard. By the way, how much Japanese can you understand?'

'If you write in katagana, I can understand.'

He told me that if he were captured he would commit hara-kiri. He said:

'If I am captured by the enemy it will be a disgrace to my family. The British and the Americans when they are released feel happy because they are welcomed at home and their country will honour them, but we suffer shame when we face our families again.'

I received a postcard from him after he had arrived at Bukit

Tinggi and later I heard that he was interned somewhere near Singapore. Whether he ever committed hara-kiri, I do not know.

In August 1944 I was talking to Morita San, the head of the factory. He said:

'There will be an exercise at Bukit Tinggi tomorrow and you will see a lot of planes; some may even fly over Indaroeng.'

He smiled proudly as he spoke of his country's air force.

* * *

A group of Japanese stood in front of the factory gazing intently towards the sky. Smiling, one said:

'Lim San, look at our beautiful planes.'

'Where?'

'There,' he pointed.

I excused myself and hurried to our house. I felt uneasy; for by this time I knew the shape and sound of Japanese planes and I was sure that those I had seen and heard were not Japanese. Yet I dared not enter an air-raid trench for if they turned out to be Allied planes I should be accused of being a spy with prior knowledge of their movements. Hurriedly I changed and shouted to our servant to get breakfast ready for me. I was tying my shoelace when the first bomb dropped. I dived into the air-raid trench and our servant fell in on top of me. Many planes flew past and dust and cement swept over us in a hurricane. Then I heard someone shouting: '*Nona* Janet.' It was my neighbour's daughter. Her mother and her youngest sister had gone to the market and her father was away. I summoned what little courage I had left and dashed across the road to the house. The eldest daughter aged twelve was cooking, the second child was having her bath and the third child, a boy of five, was still in bed. I dragged the whole lot to the trench. The bombing lasted for about ten minutes, then there was an interval and it started again.

When I thought that it was safe to get out I found that I was covered in mud. Dazed, I staggered towards the clinic and prepared to receive the casualties which I knew would soon pour in. Then I heard Doris calling:

'Janet, are you alive? Where are you?'

'Oh, Doris, thank God you are safe.'

There was no time for further comment for the first casualties were arriving. All the office staff offered to help us. Every inch of the floor was taken up and we had to spread the wounded far outside the clinic. There were not enough drugs but we did our best; the dead were separated from the living. Later, two military doctors, drugs and an ambulance arrived from Padang and those patients who had any hope of recovery were transferred there. About sixty were very seriously wounded; in addition, many had been killed and a few buried alive. All the casualties were Malay or Chinese coolies except for two Japanese civilians and two Japanese soldiers. When the last casualties had been attended to

I nearly fainted, and found, to my surprise, that it was already 4 p.m. I realised that I had not yet had breakfast. Feeling miserable and exhausted, I left the clinic and found to my dismay that my room had collapsed. With no bed to rest on and no clothes to change into I was close to tears. Then a knock brought me to my feet. The chief cashier stood at the door looking rather sad.

'Miss Lim, our cow has been killed by the Americans.' Doris burst out laughing.

'Don't tell me that the Americans came all that way just to kill your cow.'

Not long before, the chief cashier had asked me if I would like to join him in buying a cow as milk was so difficult to get. The particular cow he had in mind cost eight hundred guilders and four of us contributed to this sum. When our cow arrived she was honoured by a large crowd of people who turned out to welcome her to the factory. She looked wild and vicious and I had doubts as to whether I could manage her. She was housed in an attap hut behind the clinic and every fourth day it was my turn to take her out grazing. The cow and I trod slowly through the village and sometimes past the office of the factory. The Japanese would pop their heads out of their office and smile, while the coolies called out 'cow girl'. However, I did not mind because I thought that I would soon get some milk, but alas, the long-awaited milk never seemed to come, although the seller had sworn when we bought her that she was in calf. I shed tears when the cashier told me of this casualty. Later the carcass was divided into four portions and we had meat to eat for weeks on end.

Many unexploded bombs lay scattered all over Indaroeng. Surprisingly, the factory was not damaged much, but enough to put it out of action for a few weeks. The harbour suffered more, as a ship loaded with cement had received a direct hit and there had been many casualties. The bombing had also damaged all the water pipes in the village and for a while we had to carry water from the mountain streams. The Japanese were determined to get the factory in working order quickly. They searched for labourers in all the villages, even those as far off as Sawah-Loento, and within a short period 4,000 coolies were brought to Indaroeng. They were very unhealthy, and many of them had dirty sores and ulcers all over their bodies. It was a tedious enough job to get them clean, let alone to keep them well. Slowly the damaged pipes and houses were repaired and the fear of another attack seemed to disappear; but Doris and I did not discount the possibility for we thought that the Allies would surely come back as soon as they knew that the factory was in working order again. The Japanese knew that the Allies were keeping a close watch on it. 'Cement is very important in war,' one of the Japanese told me, a fact that had never occurred to me. Doris suggested that we should resign from the clinic as soon as we knew that the factory had been repaired, but I told her that we would need a good reason for resigning.

There were persistent rumours in Padang that the military police had a black list of people suspected of being Allied spies and we did not want to get on to it. Doris agreed; she lived in terror of being taken for a spy because she had seen what happened to spies in China. I made some inquiries through friends to find out whether our names were already on the list. Apparently they were not. However, Doris was not satisfied and said that she would try to think of some scheme which would enable her to leave Indaroeng.

Personally, I was happy there. I had interesting work to keep me occupied and I thought that if I were going to be killed it might as well be at Indaroeng as anywhere else. Apart from the noise and the dust of the factory, Indaroeng stood in lovely surroundings. Moreover, I liked the villagers though their carefree attitude worried me. They would not work if they had enough to eat for the next day. For instance, one day I met the father of a family wandering aimlessly around the village and I asked him why he was not at work. He told me proudly that he had won a few guilders at cockfighting and he reckoned that the money would last his family for some days, so he was taking a rest. I scolded him.

'Don't you ever save? Suppose you should become ill and be unable to earn. What would happen to your children?'

He smiled. He had enough money for a few days and that was all he cared about.

As time went on, conditions became more difficult. Food was hard to get and expensive, so Doris and I decided to keep poultry. We each bought a pair of geese and ten chickens and, in addition, I bought fourteen ducks. I had no idea how to choose them. When the flock of ducks arrived I noticed a fat one which I was told by the owner would soon lay eggs. Actually it had a tumour and was well on its way to the grave. When I fed them I noticed two of them standing aside waiting for the rest to finish feeding. The seller said that these were male ducks and had been taught to behave like gentlemen! I was furious when I discovered that one was lame and the other blind. The blind duck was always left behind by her companions and when she discovered it, quacked loudly. Doris used to tease me and say that I should take my ducks to a circus. Week after week I waited for them to lay eggs but gradually, one by one, the chickens and ducks disappeared. They either died or they were eaten by snakes. Most of these snakes were harmless but one day I saw a large one swallowing a goat. Afterwards it went to sleep and I informed the police who killed it and, to my annoyance, dumped the carcass near the clinic.

The sound of sirens became quite usual in Indaroeng but there was no more bombing; in spite of this Doris grew more and more afraid and she begged that we should leave soon. Then suddenly one day she decided to marry a Chinese. I was amazed and said:

'Doris, have you any love for him?'

She looked at me in a queer way and answered:

'Don't be stupid, Janet. I have no love whatsoever for him. I only want to get out of this place.'

Argument was useless. Afterwards she pleaded with me.

'Janet, I need your company. I cannot stay alone with a man day in and day out; if I loved him it would be different. Do come with me, please.'

What could I do? Doris and I had few other friends, so finally I decided to go with her. She told the Japanese authorities that she was getting married and that I was her adopted sister and that she would like me to come with her. I felt that the Japanese doubted that the marriage was a genuine one, but finally they gave permission for both of us to go. On 28 October 1944 we left the cement factory by truck with our chickens, geese and two dogs.

The farm which belonged to Doris's husband stood about three miles from Indaroeng. It consisted of one small attap hut though a new house was being built. When we arrived we all shared a tiny room, sleeping on the cement floor; to add to our misery it rained all day and the two dogs refused to sleep outside. We had to cook all our meals in the open and before beginning to cook had to gather firewood and leaves. We visited our half-built house daily until we were told that it was impossible to complete it because of the shortage of materials. In spite of this, we decided to move in.

The house shook and swayed and only one room and a

veranda were usable. We had to stoop low to enter our front door, and the back door leading to the kitchen was so narrow that, thin as I was, I had to walk sideways to get through it. When it rained the mud in the kitchen was ankle deep so we often cooked in the open under an umbrella. The main problem was to find drinking water near the new house. Daily we searched fruitlessly and dug the ground and by the evening we were exhausted. Then one day Doris's husband returned with a beaming smile. A short distance away near the edge of a *padi* field he had dug a hole about two feet deep and had found water. Indeed, there was plenty of water, but so muddy that it was not even fit for washing. However, we got a large tin and filled it with sand, to serve as a filter, and though the water was by no means clear it could, after being filtered many times, be used for drinking. Around this water hole we built an attap fence so that we could take our baths there. Soon afterwards Doris and I set to work to clear the grass around the house. When we had finished, a storm broke out and swept our enclosure and the kitchen away. Exhausted, we looked at each other.

'It's hopeless, Janet. Oh, why did we leave Indaroeng?'

It was the first time I had seen Doris in tears; perhaps it was from misery because we no longer seemed to be civilised beings. We wore *sarongs* without blouses, no shoes and ate out of banana leaves.

After we had been in the place about a month, living on our savings, our money and provisions were nearly exhausted. The vegetables we had planted were too young to be edible and the man's wage was insufficient to keep all of us alive. Then Doris had an idea; there were still 4,000 coolies in Indaroeng and the Japanese supplied them with food. She thought if we could contact the Japanese and contract to supply them with vegetables bought direct from the farmers we should make enough to keep ourselves. The Japanese agreed to the scheme and we set to work. Three times a week we rose early and waylaid the farmers as they came down from the hills on their way to the market. We bought everything they had and sold it to the Japanese at a good profit. One morning when we were sitting on the roadside waiting, some of our friends passed by and exclaimed,

'Good heavens, what has come over you two?'

Embarrassed we looked away. Our shoes we kept for going to Padang, and the muddy water had stained all our clothes. Unfortunately our buying and selling of vegetables soon came to an end, for the cement factory, which had been partially put out of action by bombing, was repaired and then fewer coolies were needed.

Our farm was infested with mosquitoes and I did not have an adequate net. I soon contracted malaria and every second day I was in bed with a high temperature. The only medicine I had was quinine tablets which made me very deaf. Slowly I became weaker and weaker till it was agony to move about and work on the farm. Finally I could only do the housework, and the planting and digging had to be done by the other two. One day my temperature was higher than usual, my face became swollen and painful, I had difficulty in swallowing and I realised that I had a throat and ear infection as well as malaria. Luckily just then two Japanese doctors from the Padang Hospital came to the farm and saw me. Dr Nakanura had been educated in the United States and had practised in Japan; the other, Dr Suzuki, had worked in one of the rubber plantations in Malaya before the war. They took me immediately down to the Padang Hospital where I was admitted into the women's ward and stayed for two weeks. The two doctors then tried to persuade me to work in the hospital, but I said that I would have to talk it over with my friends on the farm. Fortunately I was able to convince Doris that I was a burden to them and that here was an opportunity to earn my living elsewhere. I added that I would come back to the farm for the weekends and share my salary with them. This seemed to satisfy her. I was not sorry to leave. Apart from everything else, there were frequent quarrels between Doris and her husband.

A storeroom near the wards was given to me for a bedroom until I could find accommodation elsewhere. The hospital, called the 'Roemah Sakit Besar' (big sick house), stood outside the town; it was the one I had visited when I was at the Yamato Hotel. Different sections were used by the military and the Japanese civilians, and there was a women's and children's ward which was in the care of Malay doctors and nurses. I was detailed to the Japanese civilian ward under Drs Nakanura and Suzuki; I was the only Chinese nurse working in the hospital. All the prescriptions, medical reports and instructions were written either in Malay or in Japanese which put me at a great disadvantage, so that I could only serve the meals, tidy the wards and do the dressings.

The Japanese patients were difficult to nurse. The tuberculous ones spat anywhere they pleased, although sputum mugs were supplied and they had been instructed how to use them. One afternoon I found a T.B. patient cleaning his mouth in the kitchen sink and I told him not to do it. He was very angry: 'Japanese nurse, no tell patients what to do. You, China, go away.' I decided to be brave and reported these patients to the Japanese doctors. They told me to wait in their office while they went to see the patients. What they said I do not know, but after this I was put into the X-ray department where I was kept busy all day, except when work was interrupted by visits to the air-raid shelters. Bombers often circled round, but the Japanese had great confidence that the Allies would never bomb a hospital. The doctors were very pleasant to work under and gave the same treatment to all nationalities. They had many Chinese and Malay friends who often came to them for help. Some drugs were impossible to get outside the hospital but these people seldom went away empty-handed. These two doctors earned the goodwill of the population and I am glad to say that when I visited Tokyo in 1954 I saw Dr

Nakanura in good health; I do not know what happened to Dr Suzuki.

As I could not cook in my room, arrangements were made for me to collect my daily ration from the kitchen—it consisted of a bowl of rice and a piece of meat as tough as leather. Although I was working in the X-ray department I had constant contact with the women's ward and, in particular, I came to know many patients who were 'comfort girls'. They had weekly medical examinations for venereal disease outside the hospital and if infected were sent in for treatment. I grew to understand their difficulties and problems well, and this knowledge gave me more sympathy for a similar group, whom I cared for after the war when I was a nurse in the Government Social Hygiene Hospital in Singapore.

Continued in *Sold for Silver* by Janet Lim.

SOLD FOR SILVER

An autobiography of a girl sold
into slavery in Southeast Asia

Janet Lim

'I was looked at, criticized, and after much bargaining sold for $250.' So begins Janet Lim's ordeal as a *mui tsai*, or slave girl, in 1930s Singapore. But this is only the beginning of a remarkable journey, which sees the author freed from child bondage to assume a position of leadership and obtain true happiness in later life. After gaining her freedom, Janet is educated by missionaries and serves under colonial tutelage as a nurse. Her misfortunes return, however, when Singapore falls to the Japanese in 1942 — the ship that she flees Singapore on is bombed and she drifts for days at sea. Rescued by Indonesian fishermen, she is finally captured and imprisoned in Japanese-occupied Sumatra. To avoid becoming a comfort woman, Janet escapes into the jungle villages of west Sumatra but is once again caught, and this time tortured by the Japanese military police and threatened with the firing squad.

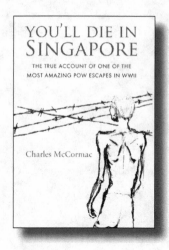

YOU'LL DIE IN SINGAPORE
The true account of one of the
most amazing POW escapes in
WWII

Charles McCormac

Weakened by hunger, thirst and
ill-treatment, author Charles
McCormac, then a WWII prisoner
of war in Japanese-occupied Singapore, knew that if he did not
escape he would die. With sixteen others he broke out of Pasir
Panjang camp and began an epic two-thousand-mile escape
from the island of Singapore, through the jungles of Indonesia to
Australia. With no compass and no map, and only the goodwill of
villagers and their own wits to rely on, the British and Australian
POWs' escape took a staggering five months and only two out of
the original seventeen men survived. You'll Die in Singapore is
Charles McCormac's compelling true account of one of the most
horrifying and amazing escapes in WWII. It is a story of courage,
endurance and compassion, and makes for a very gripping read.

MALAYAN SPYMASTER

Memoirs of a rubber planter, bandit fighter and spy

Boris Hembry

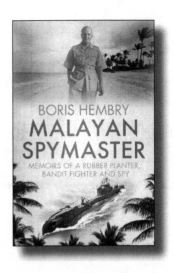

This is a true story of 1930s Malaysia, of jungle operations, submarines and spies in WWII, and of the postwar Malayan Emergency, as experienced by an extraordinary man.

Boris Hembry went out to Malaya as a rubber planter in 1930 to work on estates in Malaya and Sumatra. Following the Japanese invasion in December 1941 he volunteered for Freddy Spencer Chapman's covert Stay Behind Party and spent a month in the jungle behind enemy lines before escaping by sampan across the Malacca Strait to Sumatra. Hembry returned to Singapore shortly before its surrender then escaped to Java and subsequently to India, where he joined V Force, a clandestine intelligence unit operating in Burma.

In 1943 Hembry was recruited into the Secret Intelligence Service – given the bland cover name Inter-Services Liaison Department (ISLD) – and returned to Sumatra and Malaya several times by submarine on intelligence-gathering missions. He became Head of Malayan Country Section ISLD in 1944, liaised with Force 136, and was responsible for the most successful intelligence coup of the Malayan war

After WWII, Hembry returned to planting at Sungei Siput, Perak, where the murder of three colleagues on 16 June 1948 signalled the start of the Malayan Emergency. Assuming the leadership of the local planting community, he formed the first Home Guard unit in Malaya, was an early proponent of squatter control (later incorporated into the Briggs Plan), served on district, state and federal security committees, and survived several attempts on his life.

OUR MAN IN MALAYA
John Davis (CBE, DSO),
SOE Force 136 and Postwar
Counter-Insurgency

Margaret Shennan

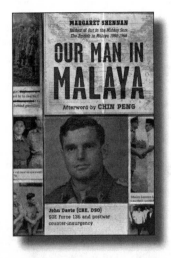

The career of John Davis was inextricably and paradoxically intertwined with that of Chin Peng, the leader of the Malayan Communist Party and the man who was to become Britain's chief enemy in the long Communist struggle for the soul of Malaya. When the Japanese invaded Malaya during WWII, John Davis escaped to Ceylon, sailing 1,700 miles in a Malay fishing boat, before planning the infiltration of Chinese intelligence agents and British officers back into the Malayan peninsula. With the support of Chin Peng and the cooperation of the Malayan Peoples Anti-Japanese Army, Davis led SOE Force 136 into Japanese-occupied Malaya where he operated from camps deep in the jungle with Freddy Spencer Chapman and fellow covert agents. Yet Davis was more than a wartime hero. Following the war, he was heavily involved in Malayan Emergency affairs: squatter control, the establishment of New Villages and, vitally, of tracking down and confronting his old adversary Chin Peng and the communist terrorists. Historian and biographer Margaret Shennan, born and raised in Malaya and an expert on the British in pre-independence Malaysia, tells the extraordinary, untold story of John Davis, CBE, DSO, an iconic figure in Malaya's colonial history. Illustrated with Davis' personal photographs and featuring correspondence between Davis and Chin Peng, this is a story which truly deserves to be told.